Advance Praise for *Create More Flow*

"As an executive at a high-growth tech company and a mother, *Create More Flow* had a major impact on how I live my life, coach my team, and take care of my family. I'm now much more conscious of when I'm in a high performance state and how to trigger one. Camille's insights have also helped me clear my mind and enjoy my work and life more fully. I highly recommend this book."

—**Leah Belsky**, VP Global Enterprise Development, Coursera

"Have you ever experienced a time when you were engaged in something and you were so absorbed that you completely lost track of time? Do you remember how productive and efficient you were? Can you imagine how much more productive and effective we could all be if we could be in that state more of the time? That state is what's known as "flow," and Dr. Camille Preston's new book, *Create More Flow*, explains how you can create that space for yourself more often and more quickly. Her work is based on recent research in neuroscience and grounded by her own experience in creating more flow for herself and her executive clients."

—**William Courville, Ph.D.**, faculty, Georgetown University, Institute of Transformational Leadership

"*Create More Flow* offers timely advice for leaders looking for effective strategies to navigate our volatile, uncertain, complex, and ambiguous world."

—**General George Casey**, U.S. Army (Retired), Distinguished Visiting Lecturer of Leadership, Cornell University

"*Create More Flow* really nails the concept of flow — that incredibly effortless state of concentration and motivation where time slips away. This book is filled with great tips and research on how to unlock your peak performance more often. A must read for anyone who wants to be more satisfied and productive!"

—**Kathryn Minshew**, CEO & Founder, TheMuse.com

"Dr. Preston has developed simple — yet powerful — tips to becoming more efficient in tapping your creative juices. A must read for anyone interested in maximizing his/her potential. Buy it! Read it! Hack it!"

—**Robert W. Jerome**, Collegiate Professor Emeritus, Graduate School of Management, University of Maryland, University College

CREATE MORE FLOW

AIM Leadership, LLC
97 Columbia St. Suite 3
Cambridge, MA 02139

AIM Leadership, LLC
97 Columbia St. Suite 3
Cambridge, MA 02139

Ordering Information:
Special discounts are available on quantity purchases by corporations, associations, and others. For details, contact the publisher at the address above or email info@aimleadership.com.

Events:
The author is available for keynotes, workshops, and coaching sessions. For more information or to book an event, contact info@aimleadership.com.

Cover and interior design: theBookDesigners

Printed in the United States of America

10 9 8 7 6 5 4 3 2 1

Library of Congress Cataloging-in-Publication Data
Names: Preston, Camille.
Title: Create More Flow: Igniting Peak Performance in an Overwired World/
Camille Preston
Description: Cambridge: AIM Leadership, 2017.
Subjects: Business, General / Workplace Culture / Technology /Psychology.

ISBN: 978-0-9849041-1-2

Igniting Peak Performance
in an Overwired World

CREATE
MORE
FLOW

Camille Preston, Ph.D.

To Mark, Adie and Pres
for igniting my desires to create more flow
and more connected time with you

CONTENTS

PREFACE

Six years ago, I set out on a mission in Sedona, Arizona. I had been struggling to start and complete writing my first book. I had hit wall after wall more times than I could count. I had started and restarted the book but failed to make any significant progress. I was beginning to believe that I would never achieve my goal. When I arrived in Sedona, however, something very different happened. Something magnificent flowed through me that was magical and captivating. After all my false starts, I found focus, clarity, and peace of mind and body. This is when I knew I wanted and needed more flow in my life.

Writing was never my forte. The longest, most miserable nights of my childhood were spent at my father's side working on essays that "I" was trying to write. It was always at the 11th hour for a class deadline. I always felt helpless and unsure where to start or where I wanted or needed to end.

Despite those high-stress, late-night, last-ditch efforts and my less than stellar writing skills, I managed to graduate from high school and get into a reputable college. Arriving at Williams College, I remember the embarrassment and relief I felt when I was assigned to Professor Clara Park's remedial writing class. Throughout college, writing was a challenge. Perhaps that is part of the reason I decided to be an art major.

After graduating, I spent a year working in Africa. Maybe I'm a glutton for punishment, or maybe I'm a slow learner, or maybe I'm just stubborn, but I decided to apply to graduate school to pursue a degree in psychology. I must have known that to graduate I would have to write and defend two very large papers (a master's thesis and doctoral dissertation), but that didn't stop me. During my first semester of grad school, the chair of my department called me into his office. He had read my first paper and asked me point blank: "How did you get into this program?"

A lot transpired over the next five years, but I graduated faster than most students and stunned every faculty member in the department, as well as my father and myself, when I was awarded the American Psychology Association's International Best Dissertation Award. In the process, I learned a lot about the mindset and skill set necessary to hack outcomes. I learned how to achieve an outcome you want in the fastest, easiest, most effective way possible.

I backpacked through Southeast Asia for several months before starting a public policy fellowship with the American Psychological Association. However, I soon realized that "sausage making" (what happens on Capitol Hill in the legislative process) was not for me. I transitioned to working for a non-profit organization that supports police executives from large jurisdictions. My first day on the job was 9/11: the day law enforcement fundamentally changed from hometown security to homeland security. This catapulted me into a leadership role. When I later transitioned to working with executives, I continued to draw on this profound experience, which brought me into close contact with professionals who were struggling, tackling adversity head on and continuing to move forward.

At some point on this journey, I decided it was time to return to writing. I began to work on three different books, but couldn't seem to finish any of them. Call me gritty or just plain persistent. At some point, I decided I had to poop or get off the pot. I enrolled in an eight-day writing retreat. Either I'd come back with a book or I'd move on to other endeavors. That writing retreat was in Sedona, Arizona, and it was the most powerful experience I have ever had of being in flow.

Some might say that I was in the spirit and others might say it was the magical mystical vortex forces in Sedona. What I know for certain is that I was finally able to focus. It not only felt fabulous to be so deeply consumed in writing, it also created something great. While I had been trying to write a book for nearly three years, this retreat was my final attempt to actually do it. The book that I wrote was not the book I had set out to write. The book that came out of me in Sedona was completely new thinking to me.

I had to travel to Sedona to create the time and space needed to engage deeply, to tap into my intuition and to let my wisdom and thoughts combine in new and more innovative ways. On that retreat, I tapped into a deeper part of me and was able to consolidate my thinking into a very logical, inspired, and timely commentary about how technology is rewiring our brains and lives in a digital age.

Looking back, my writing in Sedona was an intense experience of being in flow. It was the unique yet replicable structure of the retreat that masterfully moved me out of my head and beyond myself into a place of full-bodied presence, deep engagement, beauty, and creativity.

For the past six years, I have been exploring how to recreate this peak experience more often, more sustainably, and in more areas of my life. Flow is not just about feeling better, which means living better. Flow is not just about increasing productivity and creativity. Flow is essential for the well-being of individuals and communities. By cultivating a flow mindset and skill set, we can all spend more time in flow and spend more time feeling great and creating great things. How you create flow will likely be somewhat different from how I create more flow. What I know is that we can all learn from one another and that we all have something to gain from creating more flow in our lives and our work.

In early 2017, as I complete this book, there is no question that the world needs more flow now than ever before. Flow allows us to organize our lives around practices of intrinsic value: habits and ways of being that we have decided are important, fulfilling, and have the capacity to change the world for good. This is the belief, premise, and promise of this book.

1

WHY FLOW? WHY NOW?

While flow isn't a new concept (it was first identified in the early 1970s), there has been a recent surge of talk and activity focused on flow. At its most basic, flow is about creativity and total immersion in life. It is about finding and sustaining that optimal place where we are engaged, moving forward and loving every minute of the process. In flow, we know where we are going and crave every step of the journey. If more and more people are finally turning their attention to flow, it reflects a confluence of factors ranging from a deeper understanding of how the brain works (thanks to modern neuroscience) to technological and economic shifts to the ongoing restructuring of the workplace and changes in the nature of work itself. This chapter explores the origins of flow in detail while also introducing the five steps of flows.

NEUROSCIENCE OFFERS EVIDENCE OF FLOW'S IMPACT

As psychologist Mihaly Csikszentmihalyi first reported in 1975, flow is a truly absorbing experience that makes us feel in control even when under pressure. When we are in flow, we lose track of time, and actions appear to be guided by an inner logic. One of the most amazing aspects of flow is that it is rewarding in itself. This means that when people are in flow, they are often deeply engaged even without external rewards.[1] Moreover, flow is connected to high performance both at work and in other aspects of life.[2] Finally, as it turns out, flow is also universal. In a recent co-authored study, Csikszentmihalyi and Kioyoshi Asakawa observe:

> Flow appears to be a mechanism that has been selected through evolution because humans who learned to enjoy extending their skill through effortful action — or hard thought — would survive and leave offspring in relatively higher numbers than those whose brain only rewarded them when they took care of pleasant homeostatic needs. If the offspring of the survivors share with their parents some genes predisposing them to enjoy effortful action, then in every generation, the proportion of flow-prone individuals grows around the world.[3]

Over the past decade, a growing number of researchers have been attempting to not only study the impact of flow but also investigate whether or not the brain changes when in flow. The short answer is yes. There is now growing evidence that flow is not just a behavioral state but also a physiological state. Csikszentmihalyi and Asakawa report, "As neuroscientists have shown, we experience positive states when dopamine is secreted to various parts of the brain. Recent studies suggest that we feel pleasure when dopamine is sent to parts of the brain that are involved in passive, homeostatic activity; while flow results when dopamine arrives to parts of the brain involved in effortful, conscious striving."[4]

Likewise, a 2016 article by Guy Cheron in *Frontiers in Psychology* reports:

> In contrast to its behavioral counterpart, commonly expressed by the term 'stress,' flow may be viewed as a convergent physiological entity supported by the emergence of a unique brain state. Since flow requires challenges, it must be supported by short-term stress (the good one) that assumes physiological protection (e.g., enhancement of immunoprotection) to deal with challenges. On the contrary, long-term stress (chronic) impinges on reaching the flow state and disrupts the immunoprotective effects on various physiological functions.

Cheron adds, "Because of the conjunction of action, skill, challenge, and emotion in a single flow-state, the scientific community remains confronted with the complex question of identifying its neurophysiological outcomes."[5]

These recent studies not only offer growing evidence that flow is a real and vital part of our lives but also provide us with new insights into how to optimize flow. After all, the more we understand how the brain functions, the more aware we are of what optimizes performance and ultimately increases flow.

WE'RE OVERWIRED AND NEED A FIX

Along with the advances in neuroscience, we have seen parallel advances in technology. Mobile devices have become even more powerful and ubiquitous. New software helps us navigate space, manage time, and automate mundane tasks. Along the way, we are constantly generating data — metrics on everything from how many steps we take per day to how many emails we send. It also turns out that we are generating data all day and all night. A recent Deloitte study found that many of us are now addicted to our devices:

> More than 40 percent of consumers check their phones within five minutes of waking up. As a first thing, we check our IM or text messages (35 percent), followed by emails (22 percent). During the day, we look at our phones approximately 47 times and that number rises to 82 for 18–24-year-olds. Once the day is over, 30 percent of consumers check their devices five minutes before going to sleep, and about 50 percent in the middle of the night.[6]

This means that we have access to more data and access to more ways of interacting than ever before. If you are like me, you may feel that technological "advancements" are fast approaching a tipping point that might border on technological distraction and even disease.

In my first book, *Rewired*, I wrote about how we are living in an always on, always connected, overwired world. When overwired, we toggle between two states: frantic activity where we are doing, doing, doing without a tremendous amount of focus, and total exhaustion. Why? When we are absorbing high amounts of new information, our dopamine spikes. At first, it can feel like a huge high but like all highs, this high is also associated with crashing lows. In my first book, I argued that we are:

- **Overwired:** We are "wired but tired." We are tuned into everything, but focused on nothing.

- **Distracted:** We have more priorities than we have attention, time and energy.

- **Exhausted:** We have blurred work/life boundaries and this results in no real down time. We are working longer hours with fewer results.

- **Disengaged:** Although we are working longer hours and interacting with more people, we feel more isolated, more dejected, and less effective.

The book addressed the importance of recognizing the state of being overwired and intentionally opting to unwire or unplug so as to refocus, recover, and redirect our efforts and energy. With pause and perspective, we are able to rewire in a more fruitful and fulfilling way. The book resonated for many people. Throughout my work, I've talked to thousands of people who feel tethered to their technologies and frustrated or even disgusted with their devices yet can't seem to put them down. The accessibility and addictive nature of technology has taken its toll on what we do, how we do things, and ultimately on how happy (or unhappy) we feel. The desire to create more flow in our lives builds upon the insights and recommendations I first shared in *Rewired*.

The flow movement (yes, I do believe it's a movement) is about giving individuals the understanding and tools to reclaim control of what it means to feel great and create great in an organic way. To be clear, this doesn't necessarily mean abandoning your phone, tablet or computer! You don't need to go on a silent retreat and give up your devices and even your day-to-day interactions. In fact, as I discuss in later chapters, you can even use your devices to support the conditions under which you can create more flow more effectively. But you will have to examine your assumptions, be willing to challenge the status quo and to commit to developing clarity about outcomes.

THE AMERICAN DREAM 2.0

One thing is clear: The American dream is changing. The research is compelling.

For decades, the American Dream has been measured externally. "Making it" was measured by fixed or quantitative accomplishments: a home, a car, a family (2.3 kids) and the opportunity to retire in comfort. Apparently, the American Dream might need an upgrade. Focusing on material pursuits and accumulating wealth creates a negative return on one's mental health. Once basic needs are met (or after $75k), money doesn't materially change your happiness.[7] In fact, the desire for material goods can even have the opposite effect. Some studies have found that focusing on the pursuit of material goods breeds anxiety, isolation, and even alienation.

This brings us to the American Dream 2.0, which shifts the focus from the quest for things to the quest for personal fulfillment. In this dream, happiness is more important than accumulating material wealth. In this dream, happiness also does not come from accomplishments alone but rather from the sense that you are making progress and moving towards things you have identified as personally important.

MetLife recently conducted 1000 interviews as part of their study on the current status of the American Dream. This is what they concluded:

> Americans are less concerned with material issues ... life's traditional markers of success — getting married, buying a house, having a family, and building wealth — do not matter as much today. Rather, achieving a sense of personal fulfillment is more important toward realizing the American dream than accumulating material wealth.[8]

The Center for a New American Dream surveyed nearly 2000 Americans who agreed. When asked about their individual version of the American dream, individuals identified personal freedom, security, achieving personal potential, and having time to enjoy life as the most important factors.

Tim Kasser, the author of *The High Price of Materialism,* has analyzed over a decade of empirical data on materialism and well-being. Similar to the MetLife research, Kasser found that a higher value on material goods was associated with insecurity and lower levels of social and empathetic behavior.[9] Said more simply, looking out the window at what is owned by the Jones family next door — and, in turn, wanting what they have — doesn't breed well-being. In fact, looking enviously at our neighbors does the opposite: It drains us. So, what does breed happiness?

The best way to increase your sense of well-being is to embrace a growth mindset and to organize your life around intrinsic values — those things that you have decided are important and fulfilling. How do you do this? One way to start is by creating more flow in your work and in every other aspect of your life.

THE CHANGING NATURE OF WORK MAKES FLOW MORE ESSENTIAL

One final trend driving the push towards flow is the current re-engineering of work.

Technology has had a massive, far-reaching impact on our economy that has in turn impacted the way we work. As Diane Mulcahy observes in *The Gig Economy*, "A good job like beauty is in the eye of the beholder. One person's dream job is another's version of a Dilbert cartoon." But as Mulcahy further observes, in today's economy, "Some people want work to challenge and observe them. They derive a sense of *Flow*, or deep enjoyment and creativity, from their days and look for a job that provides that feeling." [10] Not only does creating more flow make business sense, but it is becoming a business imperative in our new global economy.

Globalization has resulted in less job security. Technology has reduced geographic barriers and increased job competition. As companies consolidate and new technologies promote more effective collaboration across geography, jobs are being eliminated. More cost-effective labor can be engaged across multiple locations and redundancy is on the rise.

New technological platforms such as TaskRabbit, Upwork and Catalant make it easier to fractionalize, subcontract, and outsource work. This is often referred to as the gig economy. For this reason, results are increasingly used as a measure of success rather than the time invested to execute a project.

Creating more flow is essential for workers of all kinds in the gig economy. Indeed, I predict that over time, corporations will adopt a type of gigging, where individuals might be employed full time but are responsible for "winning enough projects" to fill their dance card, so to speak. Of course, being in flow is also important for individuals in an economy where workers, even professionals, increasingly find themselves juggling multiple jobs.

For now, the combination of more available, hyper-focused, and extremely specialized talent increases the pressure on full-time workers to stay competitive and demonstrate value. The ease of outsourcing also offers the potential of removing workflow and staffing challenges. For almost a year I worked with an exceptional architecture firm that had more work than they could effectively execute. There was tremendous stress and strain to match the right talent with the right projects at the right point in time. I predict that technological advancements will expand the hyper-specialization of skills, increase work outsourcing, and reduce the challenges of staffing projects appropriately.

Each of these trends ripples down and impacts both how people work and how they want to work. In a competitive marketplace, individuals know that they must perform at their peak. They are looking for creative ways to excel and to differentiate themselves. This tension can increase performance or accelerate burnout. In the not-too-distant future, organizations will be publically measured (e.g., on crowdsourcing sites such as Glassdoor) by how effectively they support individual employees on everything from customizing their work environment to optimizing their performance. As more individuals pursue the American Dream 2.0 and opt for gigs, not long-term salaried positions, corporations will increasingly need to differentiate to attract top talent. This book teaches individuals to identify strengths, engage their best self, and optimize the conditions for them to be successful. It returns control and success to the individuals.

Here's the bottom line: In a gig economy, where compensation is linked to task completion, individuals know that to make more money, they need to compress the time it takes to complete tasks. The more creative one can be in identifying how best to complete tasks, the faster they will be. This is why optimizing their performance through flow is critical.

THE FIVE STEPS OF FLOW

I have now outlined what flow is and why there is a growing interest in flow in the early 21st century. Among other factors, I have shown that our interest and appreciation for flow is connected to the fact that we now know that different conditions, which are in our control, can activate the brain to produce optimal conditions possible for flow. I also demonstrated how external factors, from technological innovations to changing social values to economic and workplace shifts, are fueling our desire to create more flow in everything we do. The question that remains is how do we create more flow? Guess what—it's easier than you might think!

Based on my research and years of working with leaders across industries and around the globe, I believe that there are five stages associated with experiencing flow. We will drill down on each of these stages in later chapters, but first an overview.

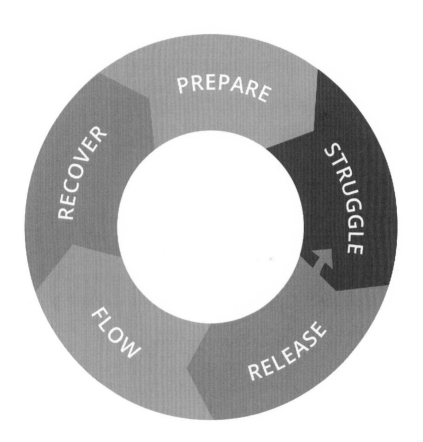

STEP 1. PREPARE

To embark on creating flow, we need to step back and get clear on the outcome. Be strategic and engage in deep thinking about your endgame. What do you want? Why do you want it? What do you need to do to get it? How do you plan to break it down into smaller sub-tasks?

Flow approach: It is the end of the semester, and Sara must take and pass her final exams. Before Sara jumps into studying and end-of-the-year cramming, she wants to think tactically about what she anticipates will be on the exam. She might make a list of missed classes and get the notes for them. At the same time, she might ask which readings are most important. In short, she maps out what needs to be done, breaks projects into small actionable tasks, and creates clear priorities and metrics.

Overwired response: Joe arrives at the office already frazzled. He tends to be so over-extended that he fails to get enough perspective to map out commitments, clarify outcomes, and prioritize what matters most. Instead of thinking tactically, he right jumps right into action. He launches into another day of doing, doing, doing with no clear direction!

STEP 2. STRUGGLE PURPOSEFULLY

Once we are clear on what we are moving towards, we engage in intentional, focused intervals of effort. This is the "struggle." In struggle, we are learning, growing, and stretching. Of course, this is not necessarily how everyone views struggle. After a recent workshop, a client emailed to let me know how creating more flow was impacting his life. He explained, "In the past, I would shut down and screw up by avoiding struggle. I was so distracted,

I felt like I couldn't take on any more struggle. But since I've embraced struggle, I feel more in control and more productive— more in flow." His experience is not unique.

When we are in struggle, we are intentionally building new skills, new capabilities. Based on your targets, this can be thinking, rowing, running, painting, or whatever you want to excel at doing. The key is to be on target: to exert effort intentionally and to get feedback. Are you hitting your outcomes? What is the next step? What do you need to learn, do, conquer, or try to move the dial forward?

Flow approach: Sara is clear about what she needs to study. She embarks on the hard task of reviewing the semester's materials. She knows herself and how to optimize her success by going to the library to focus. She lays out all the resources she needs for the first 4.5 hours of studying. She comes up with a schedule and even schedules in her breaks. Then, she jumps into studying. By being singularly focused on one task, everything that is essential for encoding and storing knowledge is activated.

Overwired response: Joe is constantly reminded of the different demands that are pulling him in multiple directions. He starts to prepare for his first meeting. Reading the agenda, he realizes there is a dense boring article to read. Just as he is locating the article, an email from the CFO comes in reminding everyone to complete timesheets. Joe flips over to complete this seemingly urgent task. He opens his messenger bag to pull out the receipts, only to see the client file his boss had asked for input on. He puts down the receipts and opens the file, just as a colleague walks by for a chat. While multi-tasking appears to be more efficient in the short term, it has significant consequences over time.

How could Joe rewire? Assuming he has prepared and knows what he needs to do, Joe could map the amount of time that he has and schedule short sprints of time for projects that are a top priority.

STEP 3. RELEASE

Research shows that we can only struggle intentionally, purposefully and with full effort in small steps (at most, in 90-minute sprints). To maximize the impact of our struggle, we need to stop struggling. Step away. Do something different (e.g., take a walk, do the laundry, stretch, or get a glass of water). Avoid thinking about these moments as a waste of time. As one of my clients says, the moments when she is not in flow are "important building blocks that eventually lead to productivity." When you reconnect, you may need to repeat steps 1 and 2 or be lucky and jump directly back into flow.

Flow approach: After 90 minutes of hard work, Sara sees her progress and decides she is ready for a study break. Sara stands up for a quick break to stretch. Perhaps she goes for a walk or simply looks out the window. As she reflects on the last activity, she considers her next critical steps forward. By stepping away, the neurochemicals of stress fade from her brain. Her brain files away the new nuggets of information into the right spots. The stress of studying intensely can take its toll, but with regular breaks, her brain knows that now is the time to recharge. Sara knows that her success in studying is more about intense intervals than working consistently.

Overwired response: Joe is so far behind he has no time to release, get perspective or even to eat lunch. He grabs an energy bar and another cup of coffee hoping to make up for lost time.

Running full out for hours straight, his efficiency diminishes. It becomes harder for him to stay on task and prioritize.

STEP 4. FLOW

In flow, we combine information in new ways to create something unique. We feel a deep sense of focus, impact, engagement, and presence. The stimulus of ideas and struggle combines with the rejuvenation of release to generate new possibilities. In flow, our brain surges with feel-good neurochemicals.

While we can master our ability to intentionally opt into preparation, purposeful struggle and release, I don't believe we can control getting into flow. What we can control is not flow but rather the conditions that increase the odds of getting into flow.

Flow approach: By clearly preparing what she needs to know for her exam and being diligent both with her studying and her release, when the test day arrives, Sara is ready. When Sara sits for her exam, there is a tension to perform combined with an inner confidence. Everything clicks into place. She loses track of time. Despite the fact that she is taking an exam, she even is enjoying the experience because she's performing at her best.

Overwired response: Rarely do people experience flow when they are overwired. When they are riding high on the adrenaline and cortisol, they are rarely able to think deeply. They are rarely able to exhale, organize, and file away what they are learning so it can then be easily retrieved at the right time. This is Joe's situation. He's floundering and doesn't know what he is doing anymore. He is multitasking with no clear objective, and he's exhausted.

STEP 5. RECOVER

Flow feels so fantastic that we can't help but want more. While there are ways to extend flow, once we are "out," we need to take time to rest, relax, and recover. Even if you don't want to, you need to do this. And the more quickly you can rejuvenate, the faster you will be able to get back into flow!

On a neurological level, in flow, our brain is surging with five powerful, feel-great neurochemicals. After flow, we can be left with a hangover-like feeling. How do you recharge your mind, body, and soul? You can — and must — do this in many ways.

Flow approach: The exam is over. While Sara isn't sure how she did, she feels confident that she gave it her best effort. After firing on all cylinders during the exam, she is exhausted. With more work on the horizon, she decides to give her body a real rest. Following a healthy meal and a tall glass of water, she curls up on her sun-soaked sofa, wearing an eye mask, for a nap. Allowing herself to recover increases Sara's capacity to consolidate what she has already learned and created in flow. Now she is internalizing what she learned from the experience — what worked well and what she might do differently to optimize her capacity for flow moving forward.

Overwired response: Joe leaves work exhausted. He's not sure why he is so tired given that he spent the whole day simply sitting at his desk. His day was a series of false sprints, pivots, and gearshifts as he responded to different demands and distractions. While his scattered to-do list has grown, he has accomplished little. Looking for an energy fix, he turns to his greatest vices: surfing the web and overeating. This feels good right now. He hopes tomorrow will be different.

LOOKING AHEAD

Reading the previous comparison between Sarah and Joe, one may wonder if there is any hope for Joe. Don't worry! Joe is not a lost cause. Joe is simply reacting to what life brings him but that no longer works in our overwired world. Fortunately, what's missing from Joe's life isn't anything that he can't generate and put into action, and it all begins with clarifying goals and planning.

Great artists might not know exactly what masterpiece of art they will create. But if you look back over time, you will see that they are intentional in their efforts, building skills, developing their capacity through sketches and studies, and always working to stretch their comfort zones. You can see how great masters, like Leonardo da Vinci, played with and practiced drawing forms in chalk before they took their paint to a canvas. Great artists often work across mediums in sketches, watercolors, pastels, oils, and so on. This is how they develop agility and see how different mediums respond as they work toward their ultimate goal.

As you work towards creating more flow, challenge yourself to explore different mediums and approaches and move beyond your comfort zone to cultivate new capacity. In essence, this is what my proposed method is all about — intentionally focusing your efforts in the right way and at the right time. This takes attention and intention. It begins with a decision and then is followed by discipline. Fortunately, the tools offered in this book are designed to help make the discipline part of this equation a whole lot easier.

SUMMARY

Flow matters and not just for people who want to operate more optimally at work. Flow is also essential to general well-being. Since the 1970s, researchers have been investigating flow — what it is, what it does, and why it is important. Today neuroscience is offering new and compelling proof that when we are in flow, we are at our peak. And the timing couldn't be more critical. With today's technological advances, we are increasingly overwired. This also means we are distracted, exhausted, disengaged, and looking for a solution. The good news is that anyone can tap into flow to regain focus and increase his or her productivity with five simple steps:

- **Prepare:** To embark on creating flow, step back and get clear on the outcome.

- **Struggle purposefully:** Engage in intentional focused intervals. If you break big tasks into small chunks, you're more likely to be effective in your struggle

- **Release:** After working in short sprints, give yourself a break. Take a short walk or stretch before you gear up for the next sprint!

- **Flow:** You'll know you're in flow because everything will be clicking into place. As you focus, engage, and combine old ideas, embrace the new possibilities that arise.

- **Recover:** Flow feels so fantastic that we can't help but want more, but resting is essential. Schedule downtime. It's just as critical as preparation, struggle, release and, of course, flow.

2

FOUNDATIONS OF FLOW

While flow might sound life-changing — and it is — all too often, the jump from our current overwired and fragmented reality to that fantasized state of flow can feel too big, too cumbersome, or too abstract. Moving from a state of constant distraction and stress to a state of flow is not something that can happen overnight, nor is it easy, but it is certainly obtainable no matter how overwired, stressed out or depleted you may feel. The first step to being in flow and sustaining a state of flow is understanding the foundations of flow.

This chapter delves deeper into the psychology that is needed to position yourself to be your best and to experience more flow in every part of your life. In short, this chapter offers the framework needed to effectively hack flow. We will explore the importance of adopting a growth mindset, the value of embracing grit, what it means to live in the "learning zone," and why this is integral to experiencing and sustaining flow. Finally, this chapter introduces the concept of hacking, what hacking is, and how it can transform our work and lives.

ADOPT A GROWTH MINDSET

Let me share a brief story about my own relationship to the growth mindset.

I went to school when I was three days old—literally. My siblings, 2 and 3 at the time, attended a preschool cooperative in the basement of a local church, and apparently, it was my mother's day to teach. A tenacious and gritty woman, my mom bundled me up, put me in a blue wicker basket, deposited me in the "way-back" of their rambling Wagoneer Jeep and off we went. It's safe to say that was emblematic of my childhood. Keep up or else!

I was at least 4 before I realized that my siblings were older than I was and that maybe I shouldn't be able to keep up with *everything* that they were doing. The upside of not knowing this is that it instilled in me a powerful mindset. I was clear that I needed to (1) keep up and (2) be creative in my thinking to be able to do so. The ever-present question that churned in my mind was: What should I be doing now so that I don't get left behind? Having worked through the emotional "trauma" (specifically, the belief that as a little kid, I might have been left behind), I was left with a profound mindset—one oriented to achieving goals.

I cultivated a capacity to anticipate outcomes and problem solve proactively. I would first identify the needed outcomes and then figure out how to get there easier, faster, quicker (or at least just as quickly) as my siblings. At an early age, long before the term "hacking" became popular, I started hacking outcomes. I became skilled at thinking beyond the moment to the desired conclusion, and then thinking creatively about how to outsmart my siblings. In many respects, this is central to creating more flow. It is about being clear on the outcome, and then flexible on the approach.

What started as a desire to not let my shorter legs prevent me from keeping up with my older siblings when hiking evolved into how to make sure I got my share of the homemade popsicles and eventually into exploring how to achieve a fair playing field at home. The disadvantage of being the youngest in my family became the training ground or boot camp for a skill set that has been rewarding and, dare I say, even lucrative. To this day, I wish I could be a fly on the wall watching my younger self negotiate "wrestling rules" with my older brother. Though he was older and taller, we were relatively evenly matched based on the rules I negotiated: He could only use one arm, and I could pull hair.

While I wasn't calling this a "growth mindset" at the time, thanks to Carol Dweck and her book, *Mindset*, I can now see that the growth rather than fixed mindset had been guiding me for decades. In *Mindset*, Dweck differentiates between people with a fixed mindset and those with a growth mindset. This is a distinction that impacts the way we navigate life, especially achievement and failure. She explains:

> Individuals who believe their talents can be developed (through hard work, good strategies, and input from others) have a growth mindset. They tend to achieve more than those with a more fixed mindset (those who believe their talents are innate gifts). This is because they worry less about looking smart and they put more energy into learning.

When entire companies embrace a growth mindset, their employees report feeling far more empowered and committed; they also receive far greater organizational support for collaboration and innovation. In contrast, people at primarily fixed-mindset companies report more of only one thing: cheating and deception among employees, presumably to gain an advantage in the talent race.[11]

We are all on a continuum of a fixed versus growth mindset or, said differently, we are a mix of the mindsets, as we adapt based on situation, environment, and challenge. Mindsets are heavily impacted by our upbringing. While children's mindsets are more malleable, we can all grow and change. As Dweck says, "Your mind is like a muscle. The more you use it, the more it grows."[12]

But how do we do this? To begin, we need to notice our center of gravity. Do we tend to orient more towards fixed or growth? Next, we can start to drill down on the distinction. The key is to notice what triggers us. What helps us to take risks, try new things, and accept challenges? What triggers us to revert to a more fixed mindset? It behooves each of us to reflect on different situations, group dynamics, and challenges to understand what inspires us and what makes us feel defensive, insecure, or fixed. When do you value criticism versus take something as an attack?

There are many variables that impact which mindset we embrace. For example, we may respond differently based on the issues at hand, the individuals involved, or the timing of the situation. Also, even the most growth-oriented individuals can become fixated under stress or duress. What is clear is that people who embrace a growth mindset more often are more likely to find ways to break away from old habits and more likely to tap into flow. Why? Because when you're in a growth mindset, you're always looking for solutions. You're already open to change. Remember that creating more flow involves being clear on the outcomes but remaining flexible on the approach. When you adopt a growth mindset, you're already open to myriad approaches.

For this reason, it's our job to be tuned into the kind of mindset we have and then push ourselves toward growth. If you have never been particularly athletic and you want to run a marathon, you have several choices. You could train on your own. You could also choose to team up with another new runner and attempt to hack the challenge together. But there is also a third option. You could join a running group with experienced marathoners and push yourself to keep up with the pace of the group's training schedule. Option one and two are likely already in your comfort zone while option three likely is not. The option that will help you achieve the best results most quickly, however, is no doubt the third option. Adopting a growth mindset is about choosing the road not-yet-traveled more often and doing so intentionally to move toward achieving your goals.

EMBRACE GRIT

Have you ever seen people who just seem to be the Energizer Bunny come to life? Even in the face of adversity, these individuals seem fueled by a deep passion and ability to consistently push forward. So, what is it that creates the determination to keep going even in the face of challenges, and even when the playing field appears to be uneven? It is grit.

Angela Duckworth coined the term girt based on her studies with Marty Seligman, the grandfather of positive psychology at the University of Pennsylvania. Prior to going to graduate school, Duckworth had been a public-school teacher. She found it curious that when intelligence and environmental factors (e.g., parental support) were equal, some children seemed to persist and excel while others did not. Certain individuals had both the discipline and determination to push beyond obstacles.

While tenacity or persistence is a long-espoused virtue dating back to Aristotle, Duckworth built upon this concept, determining that grit was the trait separating those who persisted from those who did not. Gritty behavior, she explained, is linked to "firmness of character, indomitable spirit." Duckworth defined grit as "perseverance and passion for long term goals."[13]

With so many demands on our attention in our overwired world, it can often be challenging to step back, get perspective, and develop clarity on what is most important. And even when we do, we often lack the discipline to stay focused. Grit is about commitment and endurance. Grit enables us to persist even in the face of setbacks.

Looking back, I often wonder what created my own tenacity to keep up with my older siblings no matter what was going on. How did my parents cultivate the perception that anything was possible if I was *committed* enough? My father was a deeply patient, masterful educator, and now, as a mother, I wish he were still alive so I could master his secrets. All I know is that my parents taught me early on that quitting was not an acceptable outcome.

While I might not be an expert, there are a few things I know from experience and from years of working with some of the world's top executives:

- Attitude matters: An "I can do this, I got it" perspective is essential.

- The ability to focus effort and continue in the face of adversity are critical.

- Your skill set is your friend. Proactively cultivating skills is important to build out a diverse "tool belt."

- Disciplined effort is a value. You tap into grit when you recognize it as a value.

People who are grittier experience many benefits, and flow is just one part of the package. What differentiates success is an individual's tenacity and ability to access, ignite, and control grit. After all, grit works best if you know when and where it's needed!

At this point, you may be worrying that you're just not a "gritty person." I get it! It's not exactly an adjective that most of us voluntarily adopt. Setting stereotypes aside, I'm confident that you're grittier than you think. Grit, to be clear, is not innate. It's a learned quality.[14] But grit is also not all grind. Just like mindset, grit is an essential component of flow. As already emphasized, if you want more flow, you need to understand both what you are passionate about and what ignites your willingness to persist, even in the face of setbacks. Grit is what keeps you coming back for more. Grit, at its most basic, is about the discipline and determination to grow and learn. Creating more flow is about the belief that if we can get clear enough on the outcomes and harness enough emotion, there are few obstacles that can't be overcome. Ready to get gritty now?

LIVE IN THE LEARNING ZONE

We live amid constant change. Alan Deutschman said it harshly but aptly in a 2005 article in *Fast Company*: "Change or die."[15] So how do we deal with such dire conditions in our work and our lives?

In my work with executive leaders, I often use the image of a donut to help describe the way we live and learn. Yes, a donut.

Life *inside* the donut hole is our comfort zone. It is safe, familiar, comfortable, and potentially a little boring. Conversely, life on the donut is our learning zone. This is where we grow, stretch, and experiment. This is where we feel awake, inspired, engaged, and truly alive. This is also where we struggle and grow. On the *edge* of the donut is the outer edge of the learning zone. Too much time on the outer edge, or on what we call terror's edge, and we feel stress and potential burnout. It is where our worst fears reside. Some of us never go there, but many of us do. Any woman who has given birth knows terror's edge. Well worth the visit but not somewhere you could hang out daily. Anyone, male or female, who is the sole provider for their family and who has lost their job or lost a major contract (if they work as a consultant or in the gig economy) has also been there.

Have you ever had the experience of remembering when you left home, and remembering when you arrived at work, but not necessarily remembering the commute? If so, you most likely were in your comfort zone and relatively "checked out" of the process in between your home and your office.

A mentor of mine would often say that all our passion lies outside our comfort zone. The things that most excite and ignite us come from pushing our edges, building new skills and learning. I know that I feel most energized when I am living outside my comfort zone and in my learning zone. When I'm writing I'm often outside my comfort zone, since my preferred mode of communication has always been speaking rather than writing. Yet, when I'm writing, I'm also fully immersed in my learning zone, and the rewards are tremendous.

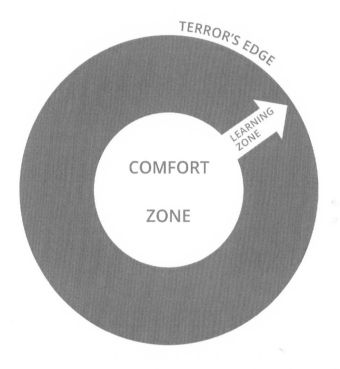

When we invest in and commit to living in our learning zone, we see that both our learning zone and comfort zone expands. Said differently, with time, effort, and repetition, what was once in our learning zone soon becomes our new, expanded comfort zone. When we see people who are comfortable in many settings, it is most likely they have invested intention and attention to grow into these zones.

We know that people who consistently take on big challenges are the ones who reap the greatest rewards. This is true personally and professionally. People who leave their comfort zone stretch themselves, constantly expand their learning zone (and thus expanding their comfort zone). People who learn to live with discomfort and uncertainty, for example, occasionally pushing past terror's edge, are more successful. Pushing beyond our comfort zones, we awaken ourselves to incredible new endeavors and opportunities. However, too much stress causes performance to decrease.

Creating more flow hinges both on the capacity to embrace a growth mindset and to spend intentional, purposeful effort to live in the donut or within the learning zone. We cultivate flow by intentionally building the skills, the discipline, and the grit to pursue growth and to stay in the learning zone as often as possible.

In the learning zone, there is a sweet spot — a spot where we are performing at our peak. Research shows that we perform at our peak when we experience just the right amount of tension or stress or pressure. We want to be challenged and stretched just enough to be learning and engaged.

Said differently, we often describe the donut on a scale from 1-5. 1 and 2 are within the comfort zone, 3 and 4 are in the learning zone, and 5 is outside terror's edge. A flow trigger is to be challenged, in the learning zone (let's say at a 4) but not so triggered (at a 5) that you are too terrified to go on. When you spend too much time at a 5, your performance dwindles.

Great leaders develop self-awareness to tap into and then gauge stress or arousal. They understand where they are on the donut, and then push or pull back to be at the "right level" of stress (at a 4). Sound difficult? It's not. We can all make tasks more challenging by decreasing time or resources. We can also make tasks less challenging by breaking them down into smaller steps, identifying times of similar stress or strain, or partnering with people more experienced or with different skills.

What is certain is that we can't get into flow without hitting that sweet spot. So how do we do it? How do we get into flow without plummeting past terror's edge into anxiety and stress? It means adopting a growth mindset and embracing grit. It also means moving close to terror's edge but without being swallowed up by stress and fear. It is this fine balance—the ability to get out of our comfort zone while remaining in control — that helps move us into flow. How do you do this? It starts with hacking.

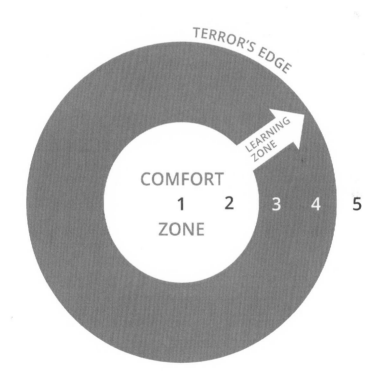

START HACKING

When I think about hacking, I start by remembering myself as a playful, mischievous little child. Yes, I'm talking about the child who never considered that she shouldn't be able to keep up with the older kids. Back then, I was clear on the outcome (being able to keep up) and naturally gritty (doing whatever it took to not be left behind). I also wasn't constrained by rules. If they didn't suit me, I rewrote them! The real challenge as an adult, for all of us, is how to return to that place. How do we become clear on outcomes yet flexible on the approach again? In other words, it is about the ability to rekindle our playful, mischievous, childlike creativity and about the ability to innovate. But don't forget, ultimately, creativity is about agility too, and this is where hacks come into play.

What is hacking? First and foremost, hacking is a mindset. It's about disciplined persistence: doing whatever it takes to break big tasks down into smaller, more manageable components. Of course, historically, hacking has had a negative connotation. A lot of people assume it is about gaining access to something "closed off" or unauthorized. I adopt the term, much like engineers have, as a playful, spirited approach to creatively getting a desired outcome in the fastest, most cost-effective way possible.

At the core of a hacking mindset is the belief that we have choices and that the actions we take can shape outcomes. There is a tremendous energy that comes from creating your own reality. Embracing a hacking mindset is synonymous with believing there are no failures — only more opportunities to engage, be creative, learn, and grow.

When you start hacking, your perspective, even on challenges, shifts.

- Challenges become a fun game or puzzle to solve.

- Obstacles are perceived as an opportunity to be more creative.

- Effort can overcome any challenge when you work in focused spurts.

- Criticism is never personal, but rather a means for nailing down how we want to improve.

- Others' success makes us stronger, too.

With a hacking mindset, anything — and I do mean truly anything — is possible. It is simply about thinking outside the box, being committed to purposefully learning, embracing growth and stretching our capacity.

In the next two chapters, we drill down on the specifics of both how to hack and how to "hack the process of hacking" with an aim of creating more bandwidth for flow.

SUMMARY

Before getting into flow, it is important to understand flow's foundations: the mindset and habits that make flow possible.

Adopt a Growth Mindset: People with fixed mindsets dread feedback and failure. People with growth mindsets seek out feedback and respond to failure by determining what they need to improve. People who embrace a growth mindset are also more likely to find ways to succeed and more likely to tap into flow.

Embrace Grit: Even in the face of adversity, people with grit (perseverance and passion) keep pushing towards their goals.

Live in the Learning Zone: There's a reason we call a comfort zone that — it's too comfortable for real growth to happen. When we live in our learning zone, we see that both our learning zone and our comfort zone expand. Creating more flow requires us to first be living in a way where we feel inspired and alive more often.

Start Hacking: Hacking is about creating habits, systems, and strategies to achieve desired outcomes in the easiest, fastest, and most cost-effective way. Hack everything and hack often!

3

HABITS AND BEHAVIORS FOR PROMOTING FLOW

Despite best intentions, many of us struggle to adopt habits that are actually good for us. In contrast, bad habits often are surprisingly persistent. If good habits are Teflon, bad habits are more like Velcro: they all too often stick to us even after we reject them. With the right mindset, however, it is possible to reverse this scenario and make good habits just as persistent as bad habits. In this chapter, we tackle the behavioral changes needed to develop good habits and set you on a path to flow. The first section focuses on mindset, the second section on discipline, and the final section on habits, systems, and strategies.

KNOW YOUR CONTROL CENTER

People with a growth mindset persist in the face of adversity. Research positively correlates both grit and a growth mindset with success. Maybe you already intuitively know this. Maybe you have already started noticing your mindset and shifting more consistently into a space of possibility. If so, how do you do this even more often?

Think back to the donut metaphor. Building upon that metaphor I want you to imagine a bullseye-like target or three concurrent rings. The innermost or center circle is *your circle of control*. Everything within this circle is fully and completely in your control. Right now, for example, I have complete control over what both my daughter (she's still a baby) and I wear.

The next or middle ring is *your circle of influence*. These are things that you care about and that are important to you. While you cannot fully control these things, you can take action to influence what happens. My 3-year-old son has increasingly strong opinions about what he wears. I can influence these choices by limiting what is available but I have less and less control.

The final ring is *your circle of concern*. These are things that impact you but that you cannot significantly impact. Continuing with the analogy, while I might be concerned about what my husband wears, it is beyond my control or influence. (Lucky for me, Mark is a great dresser).

As we embark on creating more flow, it makes logical sense to focus our efforts on the things that are within our circle of control, because that is where we have the greatest potential impact.

While you might want your company to move towards hyper-customization of work, lobbying for this most likely will not give you the biggest return on your efforts. In contrast, what is in your control is the ability to optimize your performance (do your best) and then *strive to influence* leaders by sharing how you achieved exceptional results.

A tenet of the flow mindset is to focus on your circle of control. Put the most effort on things that you are most likely to impact (your control center) and then focus on those that you can only influence.

STAY IN AND ON THE DONUT

My proposed method is designed to support you in your attempt to develop the discipline needed to be purposeful in almost everything you do: How you show up, where you choose to be on the donut, and how you get in a zone of flow. I believe that each of the five stages of flow happens within the learning zone, where we are purposeful with our intentions and our attention. This requires mindfulness.

When we are overwired, we are pulled in many directions. The mindfulness movement cultivates the skill or capacity to intentionally choose what and where you focus your attention. Focusing our attention in a mindful, purposeful way is a discipline. It is also a powerful muscle. Of course, like all muscles, we need to pay attention to our mind and keep it active and engaged.

Assume you have decided to get in shape. Where do you start? First, optimize your decision. Make the discipline *easier* by reducing temptations (maybe this means removing any tempting sweets from your home). Then, increase the likelihood that you will work out by joining a class, hiring a trainer, or enlisting a friend to walk. Create the conditions under which you feel obliged to show up. In essence, a trainer is "outsourcing" part of your decision-making process. You exert the effort to show up at the gym and then the trainer makes the right workout happen. Is this too easy? Not at all! Removing the sweets from your house and hiring a trainer are simply smart ways to put the needed discipline in place to support your decision. And while working out or eating well may be out of your comfort zone at first, they can quickly go from being in your learning zone to being in your comfort zone if you arm yourself with the right resources and techniques.

BE SELF AWARE

The final key element of mindset is self-awareness. Most likely you have been reading this book and at different points pausing to ask, *Do I do this?* When reading about fixed versus growth mindsets, you have stopped to ask, *Which mindset do I adopt most often?* When reading about our changing values, perhaps you stopped to ask, *What is my definition of success? What do I want? What would quality of life look like for me?* If you are doing this, terrific! Developing your own definition of success is critical. We each need an internal compass, a guiding light, or a north star so we can make the best decisions, engage energy and persevere in the face of adversity.

The capacity to develop self-awareness is also powerful and vital to hacking flow. I would even go so far as to say that it is essential to one's quality of life and effective relationships; it is the cornerstone of emotional intelligence.

Emotional intelligence (EQ) is profoundly important. Research on EQ shows that a leader's success hinges on cognitive intelligence, or IQ, between 4 and 20% of the time; the rest is about EQ or a leader's ability to be aware of themselves and others and to adapt their behavior accordingly.[16] The process of creating more flow is about getting you into the driver's seat more often by cultivating your self-awareness and then capitalizing on your ability to adapt (self-regulate) and to optimize your environment to create more flow!

How do you do this? Your success as a flow hacker truly hinges on your ability to step back, get perspective, and accurately see yourself. Yes, envisioning your desired self, or perfect state, has a time and a place, too. For now, it is important to see yourself as you are. Are you overwired, procrastinating, relying on a caffeine drip to get out of bed? Are you letting people drain you at work or at home? Or are you already doing at least a few things to take time out for yourself on a daily basis whether it be a daily walk, meditation session, creative endeavor or trip to the gym?

It is important to recognize, however, that self-awareness comes in many shapes and sizes. Sometimes there are quick, momentary calibrations (e.g., Am I thirsty?). Other times, self-awareness entails deeper and more profound periods of reflection (e.g., Is this the right job for me? Am I in the right relationship? What does it mean to be happy? Where and how do I feel most successful? How am I making a positive impact?). Whatever the type of self-awareness, a few things are vital: You need to cultivate ease with yourself consistently, and to build the habit of reflecting on your body, mind, and way of being in the world. As we will discuss in subsequent chapters, this is essential to triggering flow. The more effectively, easily, and often we can provide ourselves with valuable feedback, the more often we can create flow.

IT'S A DECISION. IT'S A DISCIPLINE

During the summer of 2016, my son attended a two-week "starter camp" at the preschool he would enter the following fall. Whenever we would get within a few blocks of the school, he would start peppering me with questions. "Mama, am I going to be happy? Am I going to like my new school, mama?" And so, the questions went on and on and on.

At first I thought, as a psychologist, I was exceptionally well trained for this. Naturally I responded with more questions: "Do you want to be happy at Cambridge? Were you happy yesterday?" My brilliance was lost on my 3-year-old son, and he asked more and more and more questions in return.

By my third morning drop-off, I changed my tune. When the barrage of questions began, I retorted, "Happiness is a decision. Happiness is a discipline. Your happiness is up to you buddy." I enjoyed the momentary silence as he contemplated these thoughts and started to understand (as best a 3-year-old could) for the first time that his happiness was ultimately in his own control. I also reflected on the fact that too few people, even grown adults well into their career cycle, realize this is true.

I know — you're not on your way to preschool for the first time. Maybe you're launching your first business, scaling up to go national or global, or contemplating a career change? Maybe you're just coming off a parental leave and moving back into the workforce full time? Whatever your current challenge or opportunity, decision-making and discipline are important. Everything begins with a decision, but it becomes a reality with discipline. This is where willpower comes in.

I grew up in New England where having willpower was not only a value but also a virtue. Having willpower was synonymous with being a "good girl." Here I am decades later and I believe it as much as ever. So much so that I often say — and write — "It's a decision. It's a discipline." This is what you need to know about willpower: While willpower is within your circle of control, it is finite. But there is an interesting paradox associated with willpower. Reducing the need for willpower often helps us to accomplish a task or goal more powerfully and more effectively.

Confused? Let's drum up your Psych 101 knowledge from freshman year of college! According to Sigmund Freud, our ego is the organized, realistic side of ourselves that negotiates between the desires of the id and the critical, moralizing conscience of the super ego. The more energy we (our ego) need to exert to mediate between our id and super ego, the less energy and attention we have for the task at hand. This is often described as the "paradox of willpower."

Why is this important? Because, as already noted, self-control or willpower is finite. We have a finite amount of mental energy that can be allocated or used for self-control. When this is "used up," what people in my field also call ego depletion, we are less able to restrain ourselves from the pint of Ben and Jerry's Phish Food Ice cream in the freezer or from spending hours online playing our favorite video game.

Need an example? Have you ever had an important deadline and found yourself moving to a conference room or going to a coffee shop without WiFi to focus? Or maybe you wanted to lose weight so you collected all the carby, salty, sweet things from your home and tossed them. By reducing your distractions and thus preserving your willpower to focus on the task at hand, you are brilliantly setting yourself up for success. Later in this book, we will explore numerous hacks for reducing the drain on willpower and reclaiming control, focus, energy, and self-efficacy. For now, consider just one key take away: Once you make a decision, you need to hack it to make it as easy as possible and reduce the need for willpower. Why? By minimizing the willpower required to be disciplined, you increase your overall cognitive energy to get into flow.

THE SECRET OF HABITS, SYSTEMS AND STRATEGIES

As suggested above, whenever possible, the ultimate goal is not only to reduce your reliance on willpower, but also to build self-perpetuating systems or strategies that won't require willpower and that have the ability to keep supporting you with or without your immediate attention. Saving willpower is one way we build more bandwidth, which opens up the channels needed to create more flow. Consider the following examples:

- At the gym, we can optimize fitness and preserve willpower by taking a class or having a trainer tell us what to do versus having to decide ourselves and keep motivated throughout the workout. After all, it's not likely you're going to walk out of a class before it's over, whereas when you're working out solo, you can jump off the treadmill at any point.

- At home, I don't buy ice cream so I don't have to *waste* willpower trying not to eat it. When the late-night munchies take over, there isn't anything in the house to derail my healthy eating plan.

- In flow, the structure takes away the need to be overly disciplined in our actions:

o   We commit periods of time to do thorough preparation so that we don't have to use willpower to carve this out.

o   We commit to a 25 or 50-minute sprint of struggle, which feels less daunting than a longer haul. We lock these sprints into our schedule to make it easier to engage.

o   We create clear outcomes for sprints so we can see progress and feel happier when we are sprinting forward.

At the foundation of creating more flow is building in habits, systems, and strategies for tackling things we have decided are worthy of our attention. When we do this, at least some of the *must-dos* on our list are put on autopilot. To do this, however, we need bandwidth to reflect and to cultivate self-awareness.

The first step toward creating a system to support you, however, is to identify your triggers. There are certain conditions, situations or experiences that impact us in profoundly different ways. For various reasons, some stimuli can trigger us to step up, be magnificent and others can reduce us to a mess. When we feel triggered, it can feel like a bullet being expelled with tremendous velocity and profound power, but bear in mind that not all "triggers" are negative. Triggers can be profoundly negative or positive.

Consider the following simple example. Years ago, I was living in D.C. and went out for a run at the zoo. It was a hot, steamy day when all of a sudden I was hit with profound *déjà vu* of my time living in refugee camps in East Africa (longer, different story). I stopped running as a wave of emotion swept over me. It had been over a decade since I left, but the sensation was profound. Once my head stopped swirling, I realize the heat combined with camel poop had triggered me.

Fully understanding the biology and neurology of triggers is complex. We are biologically wired and conditioned to react and respond to different things. What you need to know is that over time, certain stimuli (a taste, smell, situation) get conditioned to drive certain responses. These can be intentionally embedded (e.g., when I work from certain locations, I am deeply creative). If you're again thinking about Psych 101, yes, this is a bit like Pavlov's dog experiment.[17]

Flow hackers consistently and diligently observe this so they can identify what triggers them upward for flow and downward towards stagnation. Cultivating this self-awareness is critical. It enables effective flow hackers to create the conditions for flow and to avoid conditions that work against it. Both are powerful in their own right.

Some triggers are accelerants to action. Understanding who you are, what your strengths are, and how you perform at your best can be a lifelong journey. It can also be life changing. I know that I work best in quiet, clean, well-lit and well-ventilated spaces. I realized this the hard way in graduate school as I procrastinated and cleaned the dirt-floor basement of our rental home prior to writing my comprehensive exams! The key is that I noticed what doesn't work for me and learned from it. And this finally brings us to the question of how to develop the habits, systems and strategies required to reduce willpower, expand bandwidth, and increase flow.

HABITS

Habits are actions that are easy to repeat. They take little effort and minimal willpower. Flow hacking is all about identifying, understanding and leveraging habits to make your life easier and more prone to flow.

They can be as simple as keeping your vitamins next to your coffee pot. Since you rarely forget coffee, you can stack the healthy vitamin habit on top of this "trigger" (yes, I'm referring to the coffee!). When we build healthy habits into our lives, we are taking actions that increase the likelihood of experiencing flow. Over time, habits take minimal effort and thus do not deplete your bandwidth.

You most likely have a bundle of habits that are working for you. Are your keys in a specific spot? Do you have a pre-meeting routine? Do you have a gym habit? The more you start to look around and take stock, the more you will see what you are doing and the more you will start to notice things that you should consider hacking into a habit. An easy starting point is to notice the things that you routinely lose or the balls you continuously drop. Don't despair but rather consider these as opportunities to build new habits that will improve your life.

SYSTEMS

Systems are similar to habits in that they are intentional processes designed to optimize performance and create more flow. The difference is that systems are more complex than habits and require intentional effort or attention to execute.

If you have ever used "dummy lists" for packing, hosting an office event, closing down a summer cottage or throwing a party, you know the profound power of these systems. These lists become great systems for both capturing success strategies, reducing resource drain and increasing ease of execution. While you still have to think about where you are going or what to pack, you will be more focused and less likely to make mistakes. They also help you be more realistic in estimating how much time a specific task will take.

Another practice that has transformed my life (and my marriage) is having a sharable list system. When we use something up, we add it to the right list. Why? Because doing this eliminates unnecessary text message exchanges ("Hey, did you get the milk?"), misunderstandings, last-minute trips to the grocery store, and even disputes. In short, because we both have the right items on the right list, my husband and I not only save time but also money. A shareable grocery list may not exactly sound like an impactful system, but, as this example demonstrates, even small interactions can have a huge impact on your time, finances, relationships, and even your energy levels and health.

STRATEGIES

Strategies are a methodology that you think through to create bandwidth. They are big-picture solutions — ways to tackle overall problems or challenges.

As described in the preface, for many years I struggled with writing. It wasn't my strength, and it wasn't my passion. For several years, I had tried and failed to write a book. Then, I had a chance to write my first book at a retreat in Sedona, Arizona. It was a transformative experience. I didn't write the book I had planned to write, but rather something more immediate and more relevant. *Rewired* truly reflected my thinking in that moment and its success speaks to its impact on readers, too. What did I take away from my experience? I distilled what positioned me for success, I tested the ideas, and then I designed a perfect incubator to do it even better for my next book.

This time I didn't go on a writing retreat. With two small children, a spouse, and many clients, escaping to the desert for a writing retreat wasn't in the cards. So, I started to ask myself, what really worked for me about Sedona? Was it the landscape? The open space? The uninterrupted time? Or was it also knowing that I was in the company of others who shared my goal to write an entire book? I realized it was solitude, mental white space, and access to a hot tub. This might sound silly, but for the second time, having access to a hot tub was a key to my release during the writing process. Don't worry, I don't bring my laptop into the hot tub! Between intense sprints of writing, I take time out to release, relax, and recharge.

In addition, this time I had my editor working with me in real time, so while I was writing she was editing the chapter I had just finished. Why was this valuable? Timely, relevant feedback is a big flow trigger for me and for many people! I knew that I was not alone in the process. The criticism, praise, and encouragement helped me make progress and keep moving forward towards my goal (in this case, the completion of this book!).

The bottom line is that anything can be improved upon when you (1) foster effective habits, (2) build sustainable systems around any and all recurring tasks to reduce the need for willpower and drain on bandwidth, and (3) discover and embrace strategies for tackling even the most daunting challenges. In this chapter, I've repeatedly referred to expanding bandwidth. While you already know that certain habits and behaviors can help to increase your bandwidth, in Chapter 4, I delve deeper into the importance of bandwidth — what it is, how to stretch it, and why it is essential to creating more flow.

SUMMARY

With the right habits, systems and strategies, you can do just about anything, but there are a few things you must remember, too:

- **Mindset matters:** Develop the discipline needed to be purposeful and move towards your goals. This means focusing on your control center: the things that you already have the capacity to change.

- **It's a decision. It's a discipline:** Everything begins with a decision and becomes a reality with discipline. It can be as big as happiness or as small as getting to bed 20 minutes earlier.

- **Habits:** By developing great habits, you can reduce your reliance on willpower and everything will start to feel a lot easier and even pleasurable.

- **Systems:** Systems are similar to habits in that they are intentional processes designed to optimize performance and create more flow. The difference is that systems are more complex than habits and require intentional effort or attention to execute.

- **Strategies:** Strategies are a methodology that you think through to optimize outcome. They are a big-picture solution—a way to tackle an overall problem or challenge.

4

CREATING MORE BANDWIDTH FOR FLOW

This brings us to the next critical step in our process and perhaps the hardest step, which is how to create more bandwidth so you can create more flow. Usually bandwidth refers to the bit-rate of available information capacity (e.g., how much data one can upload or download when online). In this book, I adopt bandwidth as a useful analogy for thinking about our own capacity to take in and generate ideas and actions. To understand why bandwidth is important, it is useful to begin by considering the role of fences, filters, fuel, and friends.

Fences: In our always on, always connected, overwired world, we are overexposed and overextended. We need barriers to limit what comes into our world to maintain sanity and stop ourselves from drowning in our inboxes. While we need stimuli to ignite creativity, we want to be intentional with what we consume. Too much access, too many options, and too many possibilities can drain our bandwidth.

Create intentional fences to reduce what comes into your orbit. Simple examples include unsubscribing from newsletters and emails; not letting ice cream into your home; putting up a "Do Not Disturb" sign (even on your home office!); having clear limits about when you check your email; and putting a recycling bin at the door so you don't let junk mail enter your home.

Filters: The key to flow is being able to give the right attention, at the right level, at the right time and to the right things. The easiest way to do this is with systems that can turn information on and off, can filter in what we need and when we need it. To do this, we need to filter out things that will pull us off center. A few simple examples include filtering newsy emails automatically into a specific folder, and using calendaring systems that have point of contact, reason, and targeted outcome.

Fuel: Our default thinking about fuel is eating, sleep, breathing, hydration and so on. To optimize our performance, we want to be thinking about both what energizes or fills us up and what depletes or drains us. Too often, fuel discussions focus on consumption rather than preservation. Notice your energy level and then determine what would optimize your performance in the short and long term. To begin, schedule walking meetings or decline meetings that are not essential or that you can't contribute to fully. Longer term, think about the types of projects you most enjoy or the teams you find most energizing.

Friends: There is tremendous power in relationships. Emotional energy is vital to our sustainability and our success. Inspiring, intentional interactions can inject massive energy into our days and overall lives. Being around people in flow enhances your ability to get in flow.

Take notice of the people who inspire you to be your best. Who challenges you to the next step? Who is a grounding force? Where do you want to turn for support? Who helps you cultivate more bandwidth? Who depletes your energy? For example, after the 2016 U.S. presidential election, I knew I needed to talk to like-minded friends, so I used my evening walk to call one of my closest friends so we could laugh, connect, and share. I also avoided talking to a few friends who I suspected would not share my concerns at that specific moment.

But creating more room for flow is about more than putting up fences, establishing filters and adopting the right fuel and friends. This is why understanding bandwidth and how to create more bandwidth is so important.

WHAT IS BANDWIDTH?

Living in our always-on, always-connected, and overwired world, there are exponential new inputs (e.g., from digital devices). We are more connected to more people, to more information, and to more resources than ever before. These changes have been happening gradually over time, making them harder to recognize. The good news is that there are ways to manage this overwhelming onslaught of information by creating more bandwidth.

Bandwidth is our capacity to be fully present, engage deeply, and focus on the task at hand. It is vital to flow and essential to well-being. It is also in short supply and challenged by our always on, always connected, overwired lifestyle. Distractions and demands diminish our bandwidth. Habits, systems, and strategies can increase our bandwidth. But here is the conundrum. We need bandwidth to build bandwidth.

Bandwidth is like RAM. In computing, bandwidth refers to the throughput or rate at which data is transferred. Bandwidth is measured in bits/seconds. In flow, bandwidth is your capacity or ability to hold information and your ability to process information by focusing on the things that matter most. Again, it's about opening up enough channels to ensure flow is possible.

All too often there is more information "coming over the transom" than we can legitimately process. Over the past decade there has been an exponential increase in the volume of information to which we are exposed, the variety of forms that this information comes in (e.g., email, Twitter, newsfeeds, etc.), and the velocity at which this information is coming towards us. Our parents would intentionally consume information by turning on the evening news or subscribing to the morning paper. Now there is more information being pushed at us through more channels and more often. The result is overwhelming.

In my book *Rewired*, I outlined six strategies to manage information overload. The first strategy is to focus. The second strategy entails filtering out the distractions (e.g., turning off your devices or specific applications to reduce the digital noise in your life). The third strategy is simply to choose your friends and foes. Who in your life brings out your best? Who doesn't? Who gives and who only takes? It may sound harsh, but the more you steer clear of people who are simply a drain, the more productive and happier you'll be. The fourth strategy is to be flexible (e.g., brainstorm multiple ways to achieve an outcome). The fifth strategy is to set clear boundaries around work, life, and relationships. The final strategy is to use personal metrics to track your own progress. If you're not moving the dial on a project, ask yourself why and whether or not it deserves your time and energy.

In engineering terms, flow = volume x velocity. To make the example more concrete, let's shift to measuring the flow of water in your community's water pipes. The volumetric flow rate (Q) is measured in cubic feet of water/seconds (CFS). As it moves, this water flow is measured. Flow = velocity (speed at which the water is coming through the pipes) x cross sectional vector area (space within pipe where water can flow). The cross-sectional vector is measured $A = \pi\ r^2$ (Pi times the radius squared). Not into mathematics? Don't worry. This is what you need to know: to increase flow capacity (bandwidth), we either need to expand the pipes or we need to improve capacity by reducing the "other stuff" coming through the water pipes (e.g., make sure that only water is coming through the pipes).

Your brain is like a computer. As a result, it is also in our capacity to increase personal bandwidth by: (1) reducing noise (simplifying things), or (2) increasing your personal RAM (innovating and growing). Notably, increasing bandwidth may be as simple as literally wearing noise-cancelling headphones so we can more easily work in shared workspaces or at home. It may also entail intentionally stretching ourselves and living in the learning zone.

Think back to the metaphor of the donut where the donut hole is your comfort zone (the place where things are easy and simple), the donut is your learning zone (the place where you are growing and stretching), and the outer edge of the donut is terror's edge. Over time and with practice, tasks that were initially in your learning zone will eventually become your comfort zone. By living in the learning zone consistently, you are growing your donut (increasing your RAM). With disciplined effort, living in the learning zone also expands one's RAM over time.

To illustrate, let me offer a personal example. As part of my training in leadership coaching at Georgetown University, we were expected to take on a new "body practice," so I chose yoga. At first there were so many new poses that demanded so many new ways of moving, I felt overwhelmed. My first class was a huge learning opportunity. Now, over 13 years later, yoga is in my comfort zone. It is a place I revisit to relax, recharge, and rejuvenate. In class, I am often looking for new distinctions, new poses, and new challenges in order to return to the deep learning experience of my first class. This is why a growth mindset is essential.

By embracing and embedding a growth mindset, you don't get thrown off course when faced with a challenge or criticism. Rather, you move right into a place where you are asking: What can I learn, how can I improve, and where else can I get feedback?

Finally, think back to the ethos of habits, systems, and strategies. These practices are all about creating bandwidth. For example, build once but use many, many, many times. Each of these tactics is designed to increase bandwidth by reducing the noise of distractions.

WHY IS BANDWIDTH VITAL?

Living overwired eats up bandwidth. When we are trying to focus our attention on an important project, and we are distracted by incoming emails or a ringing phone, our devices become a source of noise rather than vital information. Because these distractions are ever-present and perceived as the new normal, we have lost track of how much they detract from our ability to focus. Here are just a few examples that surround us daily. Open-air workspaces only add to the increased "distractions." Cultures that place a premium on "responsiveness" have unintentionally atrophied our capacity to think deeply.

We are struggling to focus on the here and now. We are trying to muster enough bandwidth to execute on what matters most. As a result, we have even less bandwidth to be strategic. We have no attention or rather we fail to allocate bandwidth to what is important. We have lost perspective on what matters most, what is success, what is a quality life, what it feels like to be able to focus deeply, to engage thoroughly, to be in flow.

We have all heard stories of people on their deathbed wishing that they had been more intentional, more purposeful, more strategic in where they had allocated their attention. (As I write this, I'm feeling guilty since I have been away from my family for days to execute on this book deadline).

Although bandwidth is vital to creating more flow, it can be complicated. This chapter is designed to help you increase your bandwidth so that we, in turn, can create more flow. And sometimes, we just need bandwidth to be able to pause, step back, to exhale, so that we can embark on creating more bandwidth. The good news is that the tactics outlined next work for both!

So, your brain is like a computer, but likely a computer that is not operating at peak efficiency. You have too many programs open at the same time and maybe too many files that you no longer need taking up storage space. Maybe you are operating on a low battery, and you need to do a disk defrag. Take a moment to think about simple, small tweaks you might make if you wanted to increase your bandwidth, your ability to focus more effectively on this book right now. Maybe you can clear your desk, turn off the television, and make a list of the to-dos?

At the highest level, reclaiming bandwidth comes from reducing noise (simplifying and building habits, systems, and structures designed to give you more time) and increasing capacity (innovating and learning). And this brings me to the three types of bandwidth we can create: mental, emotional, and physical.

TYPES OF BANDWIDTH

There are three primary types of bandwidth: mental, emotional, and physically.

Mental Bandwidth: This is when you feel agile, effective, focused and able to think deeply and in different ways. You have the cognitive capacity to think. How do you achieve this? First, the right stuff is going in to your body (you have the available RAM to execute on major goals and the right fuel to get there). Second, you have eliminated anything holding you back (e.g., you've cleared the deck, broken tasks down into manageable chunks, and decreased outside noise by applying the right fences and filters).

Physical Bandwidth: You achieve this when you are focused, rested, fit, strong, energized and peaceful. This is when you have the physical energy or capacity to take something on. How do you achieve this? You are putting the right stuff into your body (e.g., the right foods, enough water, etc.), and you're creating optimal conditions for work (e.g., if you need a light and quiet environment, you'll tear down your curtains and soundproof the room or go somewhere where you can achieve these conditions).

Emotional Bandwidth: You have emotional bandwidth when you harness the grit needed to do the job. This is a more abstract, but equally important capacity to grow, stretch, to try something new. How do you achieve this? First, you tap into feelings of competence and confidence. You feel loved and appreciated and like you can take on the world. Second, you eliminate anyone who is draining you (e.g., you might put a friend who is a bit too draining at a distance in order to focus on the task at hand or create stricter boundaries with a needy mentee in the workplace).

IT TAKES BANDWIDTH TO GET BANDWIDTH

To hack flow, we need to first optimize our ability to think deeply, to be fully present and to create more bandwidth. We need mental, emotional and physical space to think. We also need to be thinking of the right things at the right time (e.g., to remember that we need to buy milk when we are at the store but not to be focused on this when we're at the office).

Again, there is the "chicken and the egg" quandary. It takes bandwidth to create bandwidth. However, there are ways to optimize our functioning, such as closing down all the unnecessary distractions running in the background when we are in a location where we can't execute on those tasks. How do we do this? We first need to be able to step back and to get perspective. And for many of us, doing this can be really challenging. So where do you begin? When you have bandwidth, focus on creating repeatable structures that will increase bandwidth when it is stretched or strained. In other words, begin by practicing observing yourself or meditating on how best to build capacity for those hard times. Still need help? Here, technology doesn't need to be a distraction—it can also be your friend!

Technology gives us access to everything (almost) all the time. Unless we intentionally shut down, we encounter a massive amount of input and a lot of it is pure noise. The Holy Grail is being able to *focus* on the right things at the right time and *not to attend* to things that are not relevant or important in that moment. So how do we focus on what matters most in the moment? How do we have the right things at the right time when we need them?

Hack 1: Wunderlist: Wunderlist is a killer list app! You can create multiple lists about various things. These lists can be sorted into folders and each list can be shared with different groups of individuals. For example, I have a grocery folder that has four different lists: Whole Foods, co-op, Trader Joe's, and B.J.'s. I know it's annoying, but true. There are different things you get at different grocery stores, and there are some things that you can get at multiple stores. Since these lists can be shared, when my husband finishes the hummus, he can add it to the list. And, even better, when walking by Whole Foods, we know exactly what we need to pick up.

I also use Wunderlist to create lists of things that I need to do at home and don't want to be thinking about while I'm at the office. I use this list for things I want to watch. I love it when friends send me videos, Ted talks, and other things they think I would be interested in. So, of course, I have a Wunderlist called "things to watch." It is the perfect inspiration to get on the treadmill on a rainy day. The lists not only keep me organized but also keep me motivated.

Hack 2: Captio: Captio is a great sanity app. With only three touches, you can open, dictate, and send yourself an email. When I am on the go, I can collate ideas, to-dos, and thoughts without missing a beat. Having a reliable system to capture ideas as they come up creates more bandwidth to focus and, of course, this is essential to create more flow. For example, I use this app religiously on my morning commute. I use it to think through anything "left undone" on the home front or to collate priorities for the coming workday. By the time I arrive at the office, I have my lists about what needs to be done waiting for me.

I also use Captio for writing. Sometimes I like to mull over an idea for a while, and then on a run the thoughts crystallize. When the moment is right, I coalesce my thinking and capture the insight. Capturing ideas and inspirations as they arise is a great way to inspire more great thoughts in the moment!

These are two of my favorite hacks, but there are many more hacks that you know and are undoubtedly already cultivating. We also know that success leaves clues; the key is to start noticing these clues.

OPTIMIZING BANDWIDTH CREATION

As you probably now realize, I am all about figuring out the quickest, easiest, and fastest way to achieve desired outcomes (and I wouldn't waste your time or energy if I didn't believe it was worth it). Also, the older I get, the more I appreciate that there is tremendous power in process. Indeed, sometimes creating more structure actually helps us surrender and be more effective.

There are many books that offer prescriptive systems that can feel profoundly overwhelming at the start. I recall with great clarity the first time I read David Allen's *Getting Things Done*. Pulling out my Ph.D. in psychology, it was very easy for me to dismiss him and his cult-like following. The precision of his systems struck me as bordering on obsessive-compulsive disorder!

Re-reading his book several months later, however, I had a renewed appreciation for Allen's logic. The prescriptive structure of *Getting Things Done* helped "GTDers" (their term, not mine) to exhale. It was all about developing the right habits, systems, and structures to manage work information. Other similarly structured systems include those advocated in *Entrepreneurial Operating System* by Gino Wickman and *Rockefeller Habits* by Verne Harnish.

Note of caution: There are countless "experts" who profess their systems for success, what to eat, how to sleep, where to sit or stand or shop! Marie Kondo launched a multimillion-dollar business on her cult *The Life-Changing Art of Tidying Up* concept. Read them, consider them, and try them. Ultimately, I want you to understand who you are and what positions you need to adopt to be impactful. While a silver bullet sells, a platinum bullet may be all you really need to continuously thrive and create more flow.

So where to begin? First, as already noted, create a capture system. If it helps, use one of the apps I noted above to help you capture lists and thoughts in the moment. Second, optimize daily— and sometimes two times daily! Third, know yourself. Break projects down into their most essential parts, clarify outcomes, optimize conditions, and minimize distractions. If you do this, you'll already be at least three steps closer to creating more flow in your work and life.

Finally, in your quest to optimize bandwidth, try embracing the following strategies:

Be quiet: In our search for clarity about the path forward, it is very easy to collect data and hear what everyone else thinks we should be doing, to be constantly confronted with distractions and information overload, and be completely overwhelmed in the process. How we live conspires against our ability to get into flow, so the first step to pushing ourselves is to actually slow down and find the space and time to be alone, unplugged, and think clearly.

Develop your game plan: Once you know what you want, you need to develop a game plan to get there. Want to be CEO? Walk it backward — what are the steps it will take to get there? Want to write a book? How and when will you work on it? Think like an athlete. If you want to run a marathon, how might you lay the groundwork for that? How many miles do you need to run every day? What is your training schedule? Think about the actual steps involved in reaching your goal and write them down.

Create metrics, and stay in the donut at "4": Once you are clear on your goal/outcome, and you have your game plan, break it down into actionable tasks that are a "4" on the donut — challenging enough to stretch yourself but not so terrifying that you resist taking action. Knowing both what you need to do and how you will see that you are doing well is important to get in and stay in flow.

Be agile: My motto is, "Be clear on the outcome, flexible on the approach." This is leadership agility: You must be flexible on how you achieve your goal. The best leaders are able to assess situations, adapt their strategy, and adjust actions to consistently target their outcomes. Things rarely work out the way we plan. This ability will see you through the many stumbles and obstacles that will crop up.

Reward yourself: Being in flow is delicious and addictive. Neurologically our brains are producing five neurochemicals when we are in a state of flow. While the brain is typically only two percent of our body weight, it expends up to 20 percent of our calories. Yes, thinking can be hard work! Dark chocolate can sustain energy and extend our time in flow. If you can't find any dark chocolate, try a donut! Notably, I'm not suggesting that you only eat chocolate or donuts. The point is that giving your body something on which to sustain itself is a good idea.

THE LINK BETWEEN MINDFULNESS AND BANDWIDTH

Meditation has been around for thousands of years, but it is no surprise that the rise of overwired living has been met with a parallel rise in mindfulness practices. As the speed of activity around us quickens, we are looking for practices to find stillness within. Mindfulness practices quiet the noise and then intentionally build our capacity to choose. Mindfulness begins with a decision and becomes a reality with discipline action overtime.

Many of these practices aim to integrate the head, the body and the emotions into a more powerful and more renewable source of energy. Each of these paths is "practiced" with concerted focused effort. As a yogi, getting on my mat is a process, a journey and a release. Like many yogis, I get on my mat and move through a series of poses and postures. In my practice, I set an intention. I am committed to a process. During my yoga practice I watch my mind wander and I practice coming back to my mat. It is the practice of noticing and returning that matters in flow too. It is all about setting an intention and then it is about building the awareness and mindfulness to "come back" that offers the greatest power to help us in flow.

Through the physical process of yoga, I open up my body and shift my physiology. In the process, many other things shift, too. I build energy in my body. I push my own edges physically. Sometimes I even do things that I think I can't do. I push my edges of breath and choose to stay in discomfort. I notice the dissonance, wanting to escape that which feels edgy and get to the release on the other side. In this space of purposeful struggle, I develop a sense of self-efficacy while opening myself up on a physical, psychological, and spiritual level.

Likewise, when creating more flow, we need to build the disciplined habit of stepping back, getting perspective, and even stopping everything we are doing. Once we are clear on our values, we can start to get clear on the path going forward. How you do this is up to you. What matters is to find some way to work reflection into your effort to create more bandwidth.

SUMMARY

There are three major types of bandwidth that can help you create more flow:

- **Mental Bandwidth**: This is when you feel agile, effective, focused, and able to think deeply and in different ways.

- **Physical Bandwidth**: You achieve this when you are sharp, rested, fit, strong, energized and peaceful.

- **Emotional Bandwidth**: You achieve this when you harness the grit needed to do the job.

How do you create more bandwidth? First, look around and take stock of your fences, filters, fuel and friends. What is their role?

- **Fences**: Be intentional about what you take in whether it is information of food.

- **Filters**: Help reduce the noise and distractions to move toward mindfulness.

- **Fuel**: Notice your energy levels and determine what you need to optimize.

- **Friends**: Take notice of the people who are draining you and more importantly, take notice of the people who are inspiring and supporting you on your journey.

Finally, turn your attention to the metrics that matter most. Know what you need to do and track your progress. This is also vital to staying in flow.

5

CREATING MORE TIME FOR FLOW

Most people I encounter are desperately trying to find more time. You may be one of them. Indeed, you may also be asking yourself, "Can I really do this? Can I create more flow? Can I add another mandate to my already packed agenda?" If you are asking yourself these questions, bear in mind that when you create more flow, you're not adding anything to your agenda. In fact, you are creating the conditions under which everything you need to act on can happen more effectively and with less effort. But first, back to the question of time. As already emphasized, getting into flow is a decision and a discipline. Structure to support the decision and make the discipline easier is vital. This is where time hacks come into play. When practiced consistently, they have the capacity to transform both how you experience your life and your potential to be impactful.

If you are rolling your eyes, I can understand why. There are thousands of books written on time management that focus how to jam more things into the time you have allocated. At the end of the day, however, we all have the same, finite amount of time: 24 hours in a day. That is, we all have the same amount of time in the day if we are all using the same, old ways of engaging and interacting. Building upon Rory Vaden's *Procrastinate on Purpose*, I believe with disciplined effort, we can create more time. Using a growth mindset that is open to new possibilities and adopting a hacking mindset, we can create more time for you every day.

PREPARE

Legend has it that Abraham Lincoln once said, "Give me six hours to chop down a tree, and I will spend the first four sharpening the axe." In 2017, few of us are worried about how to chop down a tree, but most of us do face seemingly insurmountable challenges on a daily basis. This is why preparation, what Abe would call "sharpening the axe," is essential.

As an executive coach, I work closely with executive teams around the country. On a daily basis, I meet people who are highly regarded in their respective fields. Like so many people today, they are spending more time reacting to emergencies rather than taking time out to strategically prepare for the future. As one workshop participant recently confided, "When I wake up, I'm already at least a week behind, so honestly, there's just no time for planning." If you can relate, you're not alone.

With more demands on our attention than ever before, we need to think differently. Whatever the sector, work continues to become more intense and competitive. We're expected to multitask, often all day and all night long, and to have the capacity to process vast amounts of information simultaneously. We're always on, always processing, and always reacting, but there's a cost. As described, too many of us are living overwired, distracted, exhausted, and disengaged, and as a result, it is becoming more and more difficult to focus our precious energy and attention on what matters most: preparation.

REWIRE

Individuals committed to performing at their peak appreciate the power of preparation. They know how to short circuit the frenetic overwired cycle by being diligent in preparation. To begin, these leaders get perspective multiple times each day to assess both what is on their plate and what interventions will have the greatest impact. Second, they harness the power of preparation to reclaim bandwidth, tap into their energy, and optimize performance. How do they do this?

In *The Practice of Adaptive Leadership*, Ron Heifetz describes the importance of stepping back from the fast pace of life (getting off the dance floor) in order to get perspective (look at one's life from the balcony). His point is simple but critical: The busier we are, the more demands there are on our time, the more essential it is to step back.

I understand that this is difficult. We live in a world where being always on and always plugged has become the norm. Many people can't even imagine disconnecting for an hour. Why? Because they are afraid to miss out on an update, message or call. The real problem is the false assumption that we are more productive when we are connected and available 24/7, and the resulting neurochemical addiction we have to technology! Indeed, there is growing evidence that the most productive people are those who know how and when to unplug and recharge. When we unplug and recharge, we aren't simply tuning out, but are actually creating more bandwidth to tackle new challenges. Why does this matter? As discussed in the previous chapter, when you take time out to create more bandwidth, you increase you focus, creativity, and productivity.

COLLATE

Collating is about bringing order to the chaos in our lives. Creating the habit of collating is perhaps the greatest gift you can give to yourself and those around you. This is the habit of carving out time every day to write down everything floating through your mind (e.g., new ideas, to dos, reminders, etc.). Ideally you build a habit to do this once in the morning as you transition to work and once in the evening as you transition home. I also recommend doing this anytime you notice yourself becoming unfocused or spinning your wheels.

Recall that your brain is like a computer (most likely one with too many programs open). In this first stage, the key is to capture all the thoughts floating through your mind. When you first start this process, it is hard and can feel never ending. Some people report creating multiple long lists and then marveling at how many details they were holding in their minds.

However, you collate, it is the beginning of reclaiming time, energy, bandwidth and capacity for things that matter most whether it is thinking deeply to find a cure to cancer or giving the gift of being fully present to someone or even yourself. When you download your thoughts to a to-do list (what you need to do, where you need to be, who you need to email or call back, what appointments you need to make or what groceries you need to buy), you open up space in your mind to focus on the present.

Start by writing down all your mental to-dos in one place. Take stock of what's on your list. Focus doesn't just happen. We create it when we're intentional about setting priorities and acting on what matters most. Taking the time to collate our tasks and responsibilities is a first step toward the flow state we seek. It mitigates the impact of intrusions and distractions in our always-on, right-now world of connectivity.

Said differently, collating is the process of noticing all the open computer programs running in your mind. It is about capturing the actions needed to intentionally close down any programs that don't need to be open and reclaiming the bandwidth to focus on what matters most. Collating ideas is the process of optimizing your capacity to think. Of course, to do this effectively, you need to accept in advance that you may not end up doing everything on your list.

Last year, I was working with a very successful but overwhelmed senior partner at a law firm who told me that she avoids to-do lists because they make her feel more rather than less overwhelmed. As we talked, it became clear that she was so dedicated, she felt obligated to complete everything that ended up on her lists. The same client recently sent me an email explaining, "I used to collate all of my to-do's and feel super overwhelmed. Now, I know that I have options other than just to DO IT ALL! I can delegate tasks, automate them, and cross out unnecessary ones. Delegating was always tough for me, but now I know not to feel so guilty about it."

For the coming week, commit to collating a minimum of twice per day and notice what happens within you. I recommend using the transitions between home and work in the morning and evening. Collating also can be a hack for when you notice yourself underperforming. The simple practice can clear space and bandwidth to get back in the game.

As I collate, I think about intentionally capturing all the open loops or things that are left undone. The list ranges from the mundane (e.g., taking chicken out of the freezer or ordering diapers) to the important (e.g., scheduling a time-sensitive doctor's appointment). I then think of the workday ahead, tracking and capturing important projects, actions, and opportunities.

ELIMINATE AND/OR MINIMIZE

Now we're ready for action in our high-octane lives! Before you take any action, you want to make sure everything that has been on your mental list really needs to be there. Taking a step back for perspective is a smart time investment because it eliminates clutter and creates purpose. Ask yourself the following questions: Is it important? Do you enjoy it? Will it move the dial or impact an important outcome?

Just because something has been burning up mental energy doesn't mean that it requires action or requires action now. Mindfulness is the practice of "noticing" what is on one's mind (i.e., unnecessary emotional churn) and making different choices.

As we are living in a more connected world, we have significantly more input. As a result, more than ever before, we often need to actively cultivate our ability to evaluate and recalibrate what is really important. As my father used to say, "If in doubt, leave it out!"

Ready to tackle this task? Look at your collated list and decide what tasks are absolutely essential. One helpful tip: Reframe the task as an outcome rather than an action, and you'll add clarity to your decision-making process. For example, rather than write, "meet with X" you would write, "identify critical stakeholders, schedule meeting, send meeting agenda." Likewise, while finalizing this book, I could have written, "find book designer," but instead I wrote, "finalize book design schedule, narrow titles to 4, get input from 10 colleagues, outline desired specifications for design." The challenge is to identify what you want to accomplish and to capture it in writing.

Eliminating tasks that you don't need to tackle immediately is only part of the process of clearing the deck, so to speak. A related task is to optimize by minimizing. Many of us carry a long list of expectations around with us on a daily basis. Take a moment to notice this burden. What do you expect of yourself? What are others depending on you to provide? What are your expectations for others? Take time to notice where your lists differ and then proactively re-calibrate.

My husband and I have hacked decision-making by using a scale of one to ten where 1 is not important to me (whatever he wants is fine) and 10 is massively important (I might die if we don't do this.) For example, 16 months ago, we were discussing winter stroller bags for our kids in strollers (we live in chilly Cambridge, Massachusetts). My husband felt strongly about his choice; his pick was a 10 to him and mine was only a 7, meaning if I didn't get my way I could live with it. So, we got the ones he liked, and well, they are awful (hard to keep on the stroller and nearly impossible to get the kids into). To this day, I dislike them but it was important to him to do the purchase. You can apply this to more than stroller bags for toddlers, though. Whether it is about where to eat dinner, which movie to watch, or whether to attend a conference, scaling priorities helps.

Ready to take action? Rethink your list. What can you eliminate? What needs doing? What do you feel like you should or must do? Where can you chunk activities into more manageable parts? What tasks can you minimize to make more manageable, and what tasks can be eliminated altogether? All of these questions are integral to eliminating and minimizing the clutter that obstructs flow in your work and life.

AUTOMATE

A hacking mindset is always looking for ways to achieve desired outcomes in the quickest, easiest, most cost-effective way. When you automate, you build something once but use it many times. Notice the actions that you repeat. If you've always done something one way, it can be hard to break the habit, but you may be missing out on opportunities to automate simple tasks. Take time out to see what actions you could take today that might make a task easier or more effective over time. Is there a technology that can help remove a task not just today, but for the future?

Ready to leap into action? Ask yourself: What repetitive tasks might you automate (e.g., bill paying, messaging systems, packing lists, e-commerce transactions, etc.)? Be careful not to delegate tasks that can easily be automated, and this includes shopping! When you're delegating, after all, you're often paying for a service that you could automate for free.

For example, as an Amazon Prime frequent flyer, I am a big believer in anticipating and solving challenges before they become an issue. Before the holidays, check your stash of wrapping paper, tape, bows and boxes and order accordingly. Know who is on your list and what you would like to give them, so you can search the products with the best reviews, prices, and delivery policies. Three years ago, we realized that our godson and two nephews are the same age. We spent a little extra time researching great gifts for boys at their age and then we bought three. We have also taken to shipping directly to relatives we won't see, saving ourselves a trip to the post office. By planning ahead, we're able to optimize time and resources. We make sure that our purchases are within our budget. Most importantly, we ensure we're getting thoughtful gifts for our loved ones, not just settling for whatever is at the store so we can be done with it.

DELEGATE

Knowing the outcome is important but only one part of creating more flow. After all, having a very long list of things to do is great, but it won't give you the space to think deeply and move towards flow.

Your investment in flow starts to pay off when you can engage others to support specific outcomes. Once you have increased clarity about the results and sub-steps to get there, take time to think who else can handle these tasks to give you more bandwidth. Now you're free to be creative and flexible in how you achieve them. The goal is to deliver the targeted outcomes by using the fastest, easiest, most cost-effective and high-quality options available.

I consistently come across professionals doing more things on their own than they should. They invariably lament that it is hard to delegate or that others don't do things as well as they can. But recall my earlier discussion on the growing gig economy that makes it easy to fractionalize and outsource work. Ask yourself how outsourcing more mundane tasks might free up time and be financially viable.

To begin, identify who can achieve results by doing a task better or faster than you. Yes, you have to build a team to optimize real-world performance by delegating and then looking around you to pick your players.

Consider who supports you to be your best at work, at home and in life. Too many people truly undervalue their time (or operate with an outdated or fixed mindset). If there is a task you love doing, by all means continue doing it. But, if it isn't helping you to perform and feel at your best, you might rethink how you can hack that task. Who can do it better, easier, and faster without breaking the bank?

Here are a few personal examples that can be easily adopted, regardless of your occupation and position:

Food: Buying prepared foods at Whole Foods might cost more, but if you value your time at $50 per hour, you might appreciate that paying $20 more to save you 1.5 hours in the kitchen is a bargain.

Fitness: Let's say you want to get in shape for an upcoming road race. If it takes you five hours of time and you don't enjoy researching this topic, you might want to invest $250 to either get a great plan from a trainer or join classes that will give you better results and require less willpower.

Cleaning: Maybe you love to house clean (some people do!). If you don't, outsource cleaning. Most cleaners can clean faster and more effectively than those of us who hate cleaning. The $100 will be well worth the investment, and you'll end up with a cleaner and more organized home, too. You can use the saved time to do something else that you need to do or love doing.

Home Chores: There are a lot of "things" that need to happen to keep a home running. In my case, add two young kids to the mix and the list grows. Add two businesses and a cat and the list grows even longer. I'm a person who likes to get things done in order to relax, yet there are a lot of things I don't like doing (cleaning up cat puke, chopping veggies, mending, etc.) and a lot of things I'm simply not good at (see the above example about house cleaning!). Use a service like TaskRabbit to find people who can help you hack just about any home chore. If you make, on average, $100 per hour, and you need to assemble several new items of furniture (a task you can do but often struggle to complete in a timely manner), pay someone $30 per hour to assemble the furniture instead. In the end, rather than waste 5 hours of potential work time, when you could earn $500, you can spend $90 paying a high-rated "tasker" to assemble the furniture instead. Rather than lose $500, you'll potentially gain $410. You could assemble the furniture yourself, but at what cost and would the assembly be more effective if you took it on yourself?

CREATE, ACCELERATE AND CELEBRATE

By taking time to create more time, you actually have the bandwidth to think deeply, to do the important work, to focus on being on the donut. This allows us to accelerate on projects that truly matter, to create time to be fully present and hopefully to celebrate more successes. We know how profoundly powerful it feels to be in the zone, and by consistently engaging in these steps, we are able to create more flow. This last step can be used to intentionally focus energy, to create, to accelerate important work, and to celebrate vital relationships.

SUMMARY

Like bandwidth, time is essential. The problem is that unlike bandwidth, which can expand indefinitely with the right innovations, time is finite. I have 24 hours in a day and so do you. So how do we create more time when it's a finite resource?

- **Prepare**: Have a plan. Don't start anything without one.

- **Rewire**: Notice what you are doing and when. Unplug to gain clarity and focus.

Creating more time is a tactical hack. Practiced with consistency, it will increase your impact, engagement and fulfillment. The following are four steps you can deploy to create more time:

- **Collate**: Create to-do lists often and diligently. Take stock of what is on the list.

- **Eliminate**: Clear the decks and clean house. If you're lost in stacks of paperwork, start to declutter. It may not be easy but it will save you time in the end.

- **Automate**: If it can be done automatically (e.g., regular grocery shopping or bill payments), automate it.

- **Delegate**: No one is an expert at everything. Delegate tasks that can be done faster and more effectively by others.

6

THE FIVE STAGES OF FLOW

Now that you are immersed in the foundations of flow and have learned the power of mindset, how to harness the energy, and why bandwidth is vital to flow, let's revisit the five states of flow introduced earlier in the book, but this time in greater detail. As mentioned, this book is not about how to "control" flow but rather about how to rethink and redesign your life to be optimized and positioned for flow more often. This entails finding the discipline needed to get on the donut and stay on the donut. The more often you do this, the easier it gets. The key is to simply ask, whenever you find yourself spinning, what do I need to do to get back on the donut and back into my learning zone?

To illustrate, consider the following familiar example. Let's say you want to get back in shape. You're in okay shape but not at your peak. So, you want to step up your game a bit. Where do you begin?

First, you hack your bad habits. You can stop persuading yourself you don't have time. You can stop trying to compete with Kevin, your old running buddy, who is semi-competitive and seriously committed to the sport but puts a lot of other priorities on hold as a result. Second, you can ask yourself why you want to do this. Is it to be better and faster? Or is this just about having fun and getting in shape again? Third, you can generate at least three ways to fit running into your already hectic schedule. When you do this, you're clarifying your goal, getting clear on your outcome but also staying flexible on the approach. You're simply putting the conditions in place to focus on something without creating such stifling restrictions that you're setting yourself up for failure. Know what? You can do this in all aspects of your life and work, too, but to get there, it is important to understand the five stages of flow on a deeper level.

STEP 1. PREPARE

Preparation is the process of creating bandwidth (e.g., collating everything on the to-do list and triaging for joy and impact), optimizing yourself and your environment, and developing a game plan. I would argue it is both the most important and the most overlooked step. Once you know what you want to accomplish, you need to develop a game plan to get there. Want to be CEO? Walk it backward. What steps must you take to get there? Want to write a book? How and when will you work on it? Think like an athlete. If you want to run a marathon, how might you lay the groundwork for achieving that goal? How many miles do you need to run every day? What is your training schedule? How will you juggle your different commitments? Think about the actual steps involved in reaching your goal and write them down.

Many people embark on graduate degrees but fall short of finishing them. More often than not, it is the abstract, self-driven paper at the end that does them in. The bigger the project, the harder it is to start and the easier it is to stumble. This is why preparation is so critical.

Prepare proactively: Because we are overwired, we feel behind and the tendency is to jump right into motion, into clearing the deck and crossing off the tasks. And while the energy can feel great, do we really want to spend precious time on things that are either unimportant or not an optimal way to achieve a desired outcome?

Invest time to save time: To be successful, we have to know where we are trying to go and to have a solid strategy for how to get there. When we invest time in preparation, we save time later on by minimizing the struggle.

In the summer of 1998, I had finished my Ph.D. coursework and with laser clarity knew that I was ready for a job and a paycheck. The one thing standing between me and my degree was that huge paper known as a dissertation. That summer, my sister and I sat down and on a legal pad made a list of everything I needed to do to graduate. Some items were small (create title page) and some were big (pass my proposal defense, ethics review and collect data). The key thing is that we created a comprehensive list of everything that needed to be done. For the next 20 months, I didn't have a choice about whether or not I worked on my dissertation, but I always had a choice of what task I worked on. Slowly but surely, I crossed everything off the list and graduated. The time I invested in preparation, however, certainly paid off. I finished on time and with outstanding results.

Get clear on the outcomes: Create a list of outcomes. What are your desired results? Break big projects into smaller subtasks, chunks or sprints. Thinking through what needs to happen clarifies the outcome, and it stimulates creativity. Ideally, break projects into tasks that can be completed in 15–30 minutes and should be in the learning zone at a "4," challenging enough to stretch yourself but not so terrifying that you resist taking action.

Why do this? It helps us be purposeful when we have small bits of time to struggle, and it creates a metric and feedback loop. If you notice a little struggle in this process, you are on target. It should be a "tough" mental workout. Think hard. Write down options. Then, step away to reflect before committing to a plan. Often generating this type of list is like peeling an onion. Once you get ideas out, you realize there are more ideas and steps below that layer. Doing the appropriate preparation or pre-thinking makes it easier to stay focused throughout the project.

Remain flexible on the approach: Next, we want to optimize our efforts. What are the different options or approaches to execute each task on your list? There are often multiple ways to achieve the same outcome. Challenge your habits and assumptions about how best to tackle this project. Taking time to brainstorm different approaches helps ensure we are selecting the fastest, cheapest, and easiest method. But remember, one option isn't a choice, two options are a choice, and only when you have three or more options are you presented with real choice.

Harness emotions to get in motion: Doing things just for the sake of doing them is hard. Get clear on the compelling reason why your project or task is important. How will it help move you forward? If you can't connect to the why, ask yourself if the task is really important. If it is simply "part of the job" and not all that emotionally engaging, harness the *why* for your job (i.e., it gives you a roof over your head and food for people you love).

Wherever there is emotion, there is motion. The more emotion you can harness, the more energy and focus you will be able to leverage and the less willpower you'll need. Know why you are doing what you are doing at all times. When you do, you'll reduce your reliance on willpower. Connecting to an emotionally compelling reason for doing something motivates us. It shifts things from a have-to-do into a get-to-do. We are doing it for the reason, not just because we have to.

During my final year of graduate school, I was awarded a competitive fellowship on Capitol Hill with what felt like a handsome salary at the time. I was scheduled to start September 1. Eager to be done with school, I created even more emotion to crank through my writing. I promised myself a shoestring backpacking trip to Vietnam, Laos and Cambodia before starting the job. The sooner I finished my dissertation, the longer I could travel. Seems simple, but knowing that I had a deadline, an incredible trip, and a job I was thrilled about waiting on the other end, I was even more motivated to finish. And yes, it worked!

Create a game plan: Once you are clear on your goal and the options, you need a game plan. Looking at the different tasks and options, identify which actions will have the greatest impact on your priorities. The key is to maximize impact while optimizing your investment of time, energy, and resources. The Pareto Principle says that we can achieve 80% of our impact with 20% of focused effort. What is your 20%?

PREPARATION HACKS

We will explore hacks in greater detail in the coming chapter, but for now, here are a few great hacks to help you with preparation.

Ask yourself better questions: We were trained to accept the status quo. Much like mice in an experiment, we have been conditioned to accept the situation around us. All too often we fail to take the time needed to get perspective or develop clarity or think differently. We need to be asking provocative questions, and sometimes provocative is challenging. So, ask yourself: What questions should you be asking? What questions are you not asking? What assumptions are you making? When have you done something similar to this? Who is really good at this? What could you learn from them? How would they do it? If you had unlimited resources, what would you do? If you had half the time, how would you get it done? Where would you focus?

Optimize your energy: Different tasks use different parts of your brain. Planning uses one region and taking action uses another. Toggling between different parts of your brain takes more energy. Optimize your mental energy by doing your planning all at once, and then shifting into executing.

Be agile: Once again, remember my motto: Get clear on the outcome, flexible on the approach! This is leadership agility; you must be flexible on how you achieve your goal. The best leaders are able to assess situations, adapt their strategy, and adjust actions to consistently target their outcomes. This is also known as the law of "requisite variety": the person with the greatest flexibility wins. Things rarely work out the way we plan. This ability will see you through the many stumbles and obstacles that will crop up. It is also part of a growth mindset.

Look before you leap: Preparation creates space between specifying intentions (outcomes) and jumping into action for preparation. In order to be successful, your intentions need your attention.

Remember that metrics matter: Scoreboarding (keeping track of wins/losses) is actually really important when it comes to tracking progress. It is a way to focus on what matters most and assess whether you're moving the dial. Seeing progress is vital to happiness, too. Although counterintuitive, the research is clear: What makes us happy is seeing progress rather than achieving outcomes. Of course, it is important that we are measuring the right things. Pick metrics that matter—ones that move you closer to priorities. Avoid scoreboarding everything and every interaction.

Teach it: Find a friend who is willing to listen to you; explain what you are going to do, why and how. Simply talking through a challenge and outlining the steps you are planning to take (regardless of whether they know anything about your work) can unleash tremendous clarity. The key is partnering and vocalizing the steps.

STEP 2. STRUGGLE PURPOSEFULLY

Once we are clear on what we are moving towards, we engage in intentional, focused intervals of concerted effort or purposeful struggle. In struggle, we are in the learning zone. We are growing and stretching. In this deep work, we are intentionally building new capacity.

This is the metaphoric strength training at the gym. It is purposeful hard work. Depending on your outcomes, this can range from thinking, reading, writing, rowing, running, painting or whatever you want to achieve. The key is to have clear tasks identified in preparation that have important, actionable steps that will move you towards your outcome.

Flow doesn't just happen. We have to build our skills and our knowledge base. That's where the struggle comes in. This is about struggling against the myriad disruptions and distractions that prevent us from focusing deeply and learning (e.g., the emails, texts, calls, Facebook, Twitter updates, etc.). It is also about learning new content or skills. There are so many opportunities to be distracted and avoid the struggle. Don't justify busy work (i.e., email, texts, putting all those files away, etc.). Get to work on important things. Schedule a time to answer emails and phone calls. Schedule your flow time like you would anything else that is important and that you value.

Maintain short, crisp periods of extreme focus followed by brain breaks: Fitness gurus and weekend warriors alike are sold on the benefits of high-intensity interval training (HIT or HIIT). The research is clear: break your training into high-intensity spurts of activity followed by slower or resting activities and you will maximize your training effort. The message is compelling: with high-intensity interval training, you can achieve greater fitness with a shorter investment of "sweat" time.

Turns out, you can apply a similar training mentality to increase your productivity at work. Like interval training at the gym, *interval thinking* at the office requires short bursts of intentional struggle to improve your performance. While interval training is about stressing your body to its limit, but only briefly, interval thinking is about stretching your cognitive capacity in short spurts. Like HIIT, focused, spurts of energy at work most often achieve the best results. And just as you need to take breaks at the gym during HIIT, you need to take mental breaks after purposely stressing your brain. It makes sense: to successfully organize and process all the new data you have taken in; your brain needs time to relax. Also, make sure you cycle between "thinking time" and "resting time" throughout the project. This requirement parallels research on the importance of sleep for both physical recovery and deep learning.

Dig deep: Individuals who are most successful in this phase are committed, disciplined, rigorous and intensely focused. One of the greatest opportunities for improvement, from the outside looking in, is the intentional toggling of energy. The more effectively a hard working individual can shift from purposeful struggle to release, the more effective he or she will be at generating new and innovative solutions. Release, after all, is also integral to moving the dial on major projects. For me, release can be as simple as taking a walk or luxurious as getting into a hot tub.

Be in the learning zone: You could dunk a basketball all day long playing on a kid's court, but the key is to raise the bar so that you are challenged. You need to be stretched to grow and learn but not so stretched that you will get frustrated and burn out. Yes, dream big — set lofty goals!

Assess and adapt: While you should remain laser focused on the outcomes you want to achieve, be open to the different paths you could take to get there. In between your sprints, step back to calibrate and ensure you are on target. Be sure to incorporate interval thinking whenever you encounter an unexpected roadblock.

Get timely feedback: Research shows that real-time feedback is vital to peak performance. If you want to struggle effectively, cultivate real-time feedback loops. Ideally, you track and assess your own progress with clear targets, metrics, and self-observation. You can also engage others who can give timely, specific feedback. While writing this book, for example, I had an amazing editor working alongside me. She was there giving me feedback and sharing real time edits so that I could see that my hard work was creating the desired results. She was also there to let me know when I was getting off track.

STRUGGLE HACKS

Notice and name: Struggle, by name and by design, is hard. I am all about making it as easy as it can be, but this is not the time to cut corners. Channel whatever mantras support your heightened engagement. Just do it! Notice and call yourself out when you are not giving your all or your best. Be honest with yourself.

Capacity building: Struggle is the work. Do what you can to show yourself that you are making progress. All too often we don't know what we are capable of until we have really pushed our limits. Purposeful struggle is about exploring your edges; the more you push your comfort zone and expand your skills, the bigger your capacity. Said differently, after enough time in your learning zone, that becomes your comfort zone. It's an incredible feeling when something that once felt intimidating or challenging becomes pleasurable.

Use willpower wisely: As discussed in the preface, sometimes to accomplish a project we need to think seriously about how and where we do our best work. Sometimes it can be particularly challenging to execute on something in isolation. The simple practice of writing in a community was profound. By agreeing as a group that we would write during specific times, we stayed focused, engaged and disciplined.

Create deadlines: Pushing yourself is hard when there are no deadlines in sight. Some of us are pressure prompted. If this is you, set up some pressure to give yourself leverage. Notice what triggers you: visibility, accountability (e.g., commit to sharing sprint results with a colleague you respect), or deadlines. There is no shame in leveraging deadlines to mobilize action. (In fact, I'm doing it right now!)

Expect to be sore: While I believe deeply in not making things harder than they need to be, sometimes struggle is hard. It is about staying in the process and on the donut. Take intentional breaks to rejuvenate before you *have to* stop. Feel sore? Shift your focus to celebrating growth.

Minimize distractions: In our always on, always connected, overwired world, there can be so many temptations that pull us away from the *hard work.* Identify your vices and find a way to limit your access to these vices. If you constantly start playing a videogame when you should be working, take the app off your phone or computer.

Butt Glue: At the end of the day, sometimes you simply need to sit yourself down and do it. Writers often refer to that special elixir that keeps them in front of the computer, churning out pages. Find yours!

Tech hacks: Perhaps the best way to stay focused is with tech hacks. Yes, our technologies can be a distraction but they can also keep us on task. Use apps, metrics, gig platforms and virtual collaboration tools to keep yourself at the top of your game. In the editing phase, I was struggling to use Google Docs when my son (he is only 3.5!) said, "Ask Siri." I realized that it was his way of suggesting that I troubleshoot a problem by automating a task. One can also automate mundane but necessary tasks like bill paying and grocery shopping. Whatever works, embrace it.

Pre-load a struggle to "work on" during release: Many times, when I hit a real stumper of an issue, I will turn the task over to my unconscious mind. Stick with me while I explain. Often times we might know the answer but we can't consciously think our way into it. Other times we might simply know there is an answer and that we are capable of solving it. I will "input" a problem (the context, data, constraints and desired outcomes) into my brain and then go for a run or take a nap. While I'm off doing other things, my brain is churning on the questions. To do this most effectively, however, I need be prepared to catch the answer when my mind decides to share. I need to be prepared to stop running and dictate a memo on my iPhone or simply roll over and write it down. This tactic is part of Adam Grant's research on why there is a true sweet spot between pre-crastination and procrastination.[18] In the space in between, we think deeply and generate new ideas.

STEP 3. RELEASE

While Step 2, purposeful struggle, is all about intentionally expanding and building capacity, Step 3 is about purposefully restoring energy to be renewable. Apparently "sustainable energy" is in vogue. Well, it is not just a concept for environmentalists. Over the past decade researchers and high visibility executives have highlighted the importance of managing intensity with release. If purposeful struggle is a sprint or an intense interval, release is when we step back, restore, and recuperate.

In struggle, we are jamming new information into our bodies and brains. When intense effort is associated with purposeful struggle, negative neurochemicals can build up in our brains and our bodies. During release, we are shifting out of this state. In release, we let the lactic acids drain from our muscles and permit the oxygen, nutrients, and circulation to rejuvenate. It is when we start to clean house, meaning the brain can clean up from the struggle activity and make sure all the information is being filed in the right places and in the right ways. In other words, while we are focused on relaxing, our brains and bodies are actively working to consolidate everything that has been learned and absorbed. Our brains are integrating this new knowledge and skills into our bodies so that we can have access to it and use it. But this also takes time. Research suggests that to optimize learning, we need six-hour spaces between our learning sprints and putting new learning into action.

Really release: We have spoken about using "release" time to shift gears and relax the intensity of focus and neutralize the associated chemicals building up in your brain. When you release, are you really creating space for what needs to happen for your brain to integrate new information and reclaim a homeostasis?

Several weeks before writing this book, I had a work intensive with a colleague from 5:30 am to 6:15 pm (yes, we were literally working that long). We were at the office with coffee and ready to start before sunrise. It was intense and energizing, and a lot of work! Together, we had an interesting dichotomy. During breaks, he would really break. He wouldn't pick up his phone, check emails, and so on. He would exhale to be really present, and metaphorically sit with the past sprint. In contrast, I would use the "release" time to sprint on other projects that were waiting (responding to my team, bouncing back email, etc.).

Invariably he came back to the sessions with new ideas, new insights and an ability to engage at new level. I started to notice myself during our time together. I saw how often I wasn't fully there, when and where I was distracted, where I turned to caffeine, and so on. I also came to truly appreciate my colleague's ability to turn on/off and make the most of this approach.

Understand how your mind and body work: As discussed earlier in this book, your brain is like a computer. Too many programs open at the same time and the processor slows down. Likewise, if you shift between too many files for too long, you risk the programs unexpectedly closing and potential data loss. You, like your computer, can work really hard, but taking time to really release is an opportunity to close unneeded files, reorganize information, defrag, and reboot.

I'm not the only person making this argument. Numerous thought leaders have spoken to the importance of release over the past decade. Tony Schwartz argues in "Manage Your Energy, Not Your Time," "Once people see how much they struggle to concentrate, they can create rituals to reduce the relentless interruptions that technology has introduced in their lives," and yes, he argues that release needs to be part of this. "The core problem with working longer hours is that time is a finite resource. Energy is a different story," says Schwartz, "Defined in physics as the capacity to work, energy comes from four main wellsprings in human beings: the body, emotions, mind, and spirit. In each, energy can be systematically expanded and regularly renewed by establishing specific rituals — behaviors that are intentionally practiced and precisely scheduled, with the goal of making them unconscious and automatic as quickly as possible."[19] Release is one part of Schwartz's system and one way in which his ideas overlap with my own ideas about flow.

RELEASE HACKS

Taper: For high stakes events, when performing at your peak is vital, consider a taper. Just like athletes taper their physical activity before a key event, we should be "tapering" before an event (whether it is a race or a board meeting). This pre-game period is essential to build up your reserves: sleep, bandwidth, and emotional reserves.

Consider the following example: In August 2006, I was out with friends on a Wednesday night and on impulse, I committed to running the Marine Corp Marathon less than seven weeks later. I am a good runner and had run one marathon before (so you could say, I should have known better!). The problem is that I wasn't in great shape at the time. Two nights later, I was hosting a party and made a similar mistake. I agreed to a 17-mile training run the next morning with a guy I knew from college but didn't know very well. Fueled up on beer and potato chips the night before, we met the next morning. Robb is a great guy, former Navy helicopter medic and very serious about running. Luckily for me, he talked for the first 13 miles and had a bundle of great stories.

Fast forward to race day. Although I was much better prepared because of my decision to train with Robb, Robb was still clearly in better shape. He left me around mile 12. I passed him at mile 18. What happened? I had spent the week before really tapering — stretching, staying off my feet and preparing for the race with sleep and nutrition. As a medical resident, he had been on his feet long days and was simply too tired to compete. I have seen this time and again in myself and with the executives I coach. Entering intense situations running on fumes can make all the difference in the world.

This also holds true in the workplace. For an entire year, I worked with a top-ranked architecture firm. What I encountered at the firm were many talented people running on empty. There was, however, one exception. One of the only women on the executive team appeared to be both highly productive and respected and also one of the few people at the firm who was not always running on empty. Over the course of my time with the firm, I observed how she handled her work and her work/life balance. You know what? Among other hacks, she knew how and when to taper. As deadlines loomed, she was evidently storing up her reserves. I could see her clearing her plate, leaving a bit earlier than usual, and taking care of her own needs. When those late nights and high-stress deadlines landed, she was simply better prepared to make it to the finish line without collapsing due to the stress.

Understand how your mind, body and emotions are connected: Increased attention to the mind, body, and emotions is critical. The problem is that at work we are often rewarded for focusing exclusively on the mind (spending hours grinding on work-related projects). Individuals who have the autonomy to make decisions, however, are generally more productive. They can unplug from the world and reconnect with the things that matter most. Senior leaders who empower their employees to take control in turn reap the rewards.

Know your secret sauce: For me, this can be a multi-phased process. I need to take stock of the things on my list. I need to clear my plate of tasks. Next, I need quality time with my family. Sometimes it is as simple as a few extra belly tickles for my son or a few minutes pushing my daughter on the swing and listening to them squeal with delight. I've learned that for me to really be my best, I also need to have a clear plan. How can you do this too? Start by noticing where your deficit might be and focus on your full senses in these arenas. For me, this can entail watching a video of my daughter giggle or carving out five minutes to stretch and experience gratitude for my body. You need all these things in place to move back into flow.

Make purposeful connections: Everyone needs to connect, to share and to empathize. Rather than ignore or diminish this need, we can leverage this and turn it into a strength. Whatever your itinerary, create opportunities to connect. Supercharge your periods of release by engaging emotionally.

STEP 4. FLOW

While chocolate and peanut butter were not new, when combined together in a new way, they created the unique taste of a Reese's Peanut Butter Cup. It's a similar experience in flow. In flow, we feel a deep sense of focus, impact, engagement and presence. During flow, the stimulus of new ideas built through purposeful struggle combine with the rejuvenation and re-organization of release to generate new ideas and new possibilities.

Feel the flow: Innovation is a bit like the commercial in which two roller skaters collide — one with peanut butter and one with chocolate in hand. Innovation happens when two ideas collide in a way that creates a new possibility. Injecting new information, new theory, and new science during the phase of purposeful struggle and carving out time to release will increase the amount of time you are in flow and as a result, increase your return on investment too.

FLOW HACKS

Be here now: Flow only happens when you are in the present. In fact, that is the very nature of flow. If you are worrying about the past or planning for the future, you won't get into flow. Optimize your likelihood of getting in flow by setting clear goals (e.g., "Today I want to accomplish X"), by removing distractions (e.g., close your door, turn off your phone, and tell people not to disturb you) and by optimizing your environment (e.g., spend more time in sunshine, listening to music, etc.). If an anxious or stressful thought pops into your head, write it down and put it aside for later. Minimize distractions so you stay in the present and stay in flow.

Flow begets more flow: Flow is like a muscle or habit; it gets easier over time. The more you train your brain to get into and stay in flow, the easier it becomes to get there. So, if you crave more flow at work, spend more time on weekends in flow doing what you love—gardening, cooking, dancing, or whatever it happens to be. The more we experience flow anywhere, the easier it becomes to experience flow in other realms of life. But the opposite is also true —if you aren't in the flow at home you won't be in flow at work. Structuring your life for more flow means that if you feel better and perform better at home, you will feel better and perform better at work, and vice versa. That's why practicing your flow in all aspects of your life is critical. A few essential things to remember:

- Dark chocolate: Guess what? It's associated with prolonging flow, so indulge!

- Leverage triggers: Sound, light, and scents—whatever works for you, turn it on!

- Time flex: When you are in flow, you want to be able to shift meetings and commitments to elongate the process.

STEP 5. RECOVER

This brings us to the final stage of flow—recovery! The neurochemical high of the flow state is often followed by a darker, drained low state. As the surge of neurochemicals fade, we are often left with a funky set of emotions. Fortunately, there are certain tangible steps we can take to manage this state, thereby optimizing conditions and speeding our ability to move through this as quickly and efficiently as possible.

Integration: Flow feels so fantastic that we can't help but want more. While there are ways to extend flow, once we are "out," we need to take time to rest, relax and recover. Even if you don't want to, you need to do this. And the more quickly you can rejuvenate, the faster you will be able to get back into flow! Flow creates new insights and on a physiological level, it creates new neural networks. Recovery is vital to consolidate and engage these insights and hardwired connections further. Integrate recovery into your cycle.

Unplug, unwire, and unwind: The struggle to recover will be a lot less difficult if you actually disconnect. Sustaining peak delivery that occurs from flow is about taking time to unplug from the stress and strain, to unwire from our technology and devices, and to truly let ourselves unwind. When we do, we change the way our brains operate, we change our neurochemistry, and we shift the way we think. Then and only then can we enter flow. So, unplug from your gadgets. Move away from the distractions. Shift your attention and energy so you can get into your flow.

Embrace the funk of recovery: Flow is draining. During flow our brains go crazy, producing neurochemicals to create the hyper-focused, creative, expansive state. As the neurochemicals recede, don't expect to feel great. Sleep, sunshine, and nutrition are essential, so when you're out of your flow, go for a walk in the sun and then take a rest. And rather than lamenting that the flow state has ended, enjoy your period of recovery. Your brain needs the rest. Relax and rejuvenate. You won't be able to get back into flow if you don't.

Manage and minimize the "funk": We all experience times of extreme overload and low productivity. Sometimes it can be managed and sometimes it overwhelms us. When we get overwhelmed, there are still ways to cope. It starts with having the needed bandwidth to face what is coming and to triage (respond to the crisis). My magic triad for getting "out of a funk" is reaching out to three people I love, getting a good night's sleep, and getting in a good workout, preferably a run outside in the sunshine.

Anticipate and leverage stress: Once you've recovered, try to make sense of what just happened and learn from the experience. Ideally, we want to anticipate stress and find ways to leverage it (e.g., if you work best under pressure, you don't want to eliminate stress but rather find ways to optimize it). Know your stress triggers and how to recalibrate.

RECOVERY HACKS

Chunk time: Just as you might create "space" for workflow, juggle tasks. Think about how you might schedule chunks of time for recovery.

Engage in bodywork: Schedule time for this work. Better yet, delegate the scheduling to someone on your team! The more options for what this looks like the better (e.g., yoga classes, acupuncture, etc.).

Create clear language: Have a way of describing what you need and what you are doing so people don't accuse you of simply slacking. Sometimes recovery is the hardest part to explain and to justify. Give yourself full permission to go there.

Build your team: One of my "besties" knows me really well. He can hear when I'm in my funk (sometimes before I can), he knows what to suggest, and it invariably comes back to sleeping and getting back into my body. Assemble a supportive team around you and ideally, a team that appreciates and values recovery.

Celebrate the successes of flow: Don't forget to celebrate the fact that you got into flow. It doesn't matter that it's gone now. You got there and you'll be back! Flow begets more flow!

SUMMARY

If you want to get into flow and stay in flow, it is important to understand what flow is and how to tap into flow. This is why, throughout the book, I continue to return to flow's five stages:

- **Prepare**: Have a road map before you set out on the journey. Creating small quantifiable subtasks is essential.

- **Struggle:** Think about interval training at the gym. It's structured around short sprints followed by periods of rest. Why? Because there's growing evidence that this method yields better results faster. Now put this struggle into your mental workouts, too. Push yourself as hard as you can for short periods of time. How long is a sprint? On a treadmill, a sprint may be only 2 minutes long. At work, sprints are generally 30 minutes to 2 hours, but rarely longer.

- **Release:** You can't sprint without release. Build short breaks into your sprints to ensure you have the energy and focus to keep getting back on the donut.

- **Flow**: Get into flow! Love every moment of what you are doing and moving towards.

- **Recover**: Sleep, take a long hot bath, enjoy time with family and friends. Recover fully by taking care of your body and soul on every level.

FLOW HACKING

By now you are hopefully already deeply engaged and invested in cultivating self-awareness. Hopefully the more you know yourself, the more you can adapt your actions to be more effective. This is an iterative process rather than a one-time investment. Rarely do we get it right the first time, but hopefully the process becomes an inspiring and empowering way of being. In an ideal world, this cultivates self-efficacy or a belief in your ability to succeed in specific situations. Living in the learning zone is all about growing and challenging yourself. Learning. It is about stretching yourself to be successful and to build self-efficacy.

By owning that, we are more in control of our environment. Over time we become more motivated in this self-reinforcing loop. The higher your self-efficacy, the more likely you are to put in effort and to persist, which in turn increases your likelihood of being successful. This is grit in action! By trying to do things that are doable (at a 4 on the learning zone), we create a reinforcing loop. But how do we do this and do this consistently?

In one of my training workshops several years ago, a participant said, "What gets measured, gets managed; what gets managed, gets done." I couldn't agree more. If you want to ensure something happens, you must set up metrics by which to measure it. This entire section is about noticing and assessing what works and what doesn't work. In what follows, I give you the basics to carry out a series of mini-experiments designed to inspire you to re-think how you do things. The goal is simple: to notice where you might have an unintentionally *fixed* mindset and to reflect on ways you could be optimizing your ability to *get in the zone*.

OPTIMAL CONDITIONS

This section peels back the layers to uncover both what is important to you and how to clarify what works best for you, so you can cultivate a reinforcing loop of self-efficacy. The more we can optimize conditions, the more we reduce the temptations and distractions, which in turn makes it easier for us to become effective. Here the goal is to help you understand the internal/external conditions that can help fuel you to be most effective and minimize your reliance on willpower.

When we think about fuel, too often we default to our eating, sleep, breathing, and hydration habits. While these are vital, this reflects a fixed mindset of possibility. To optimize our performance, we want to be thinking about both what energizes or fills us up (e.g., people, environments, type of work , etc.) and what depletes or drains us. This means becoming deeply attuned to what is internal (within us) and external (in our environment). After all, both internal and external forces help to position us to be our very best! To optimize conditions for flow we need the ability to focus our attention deeply, to concentrate on what matters most, and to more purposefully pursue the goals we have established. We need the right ratio of challenge to skill. Most important, however, is our capacity to be inspired and nurtured by our environment.

In Chapter 1, we talked about the importance of self-awareness (knowing why you are pursuing a specific goal). We also explored why mindset really does matter. Now I want to build on what you've already learned, sharing additional nuggets and exploring new approaches to innovating. There are numerous experts who write exclusively on this topic. Here I just want to begin stimulating your thinking about what all this means and what questions to start asking.

OPTIMAL WORKSPACE

This is both the environment around you and your individual workstation. What positions you to be and do your best is deeply personal. I hope by now I have convinced you of both the benefits of observing yourself at your best and experimenting with different conditions. Take stock. What is ideal about your working situation and what needs to change (e.g., setting, noise, energy, light, smells, etc.)?

Maybe you notice that you have different types of work (e.g., some work that requires deeper, focused thinking and other work that is less taxing but requires you to keep moving forward quickly). Maybe you notice the importance of pushing forward as a way of increasing tension and making the easy tasks a little more challenging and a bit more interesting.

I have a desk at a co-working space four blocks from my home. It is the perfect distance to get fresh air while mentally shifting gears between the personal and professional. This space is unique in that there are four different types of spaces within it: a cafe, a study, the commons, and the switchboard. While the study is dead silent, the switchboard is full of chatter. Over the past month, I have experimented with working from home and in different spaces at the office. I've tried different desks (e.g., sitting, standing, individual stand alone, bench, dinner table, etc.); different environments (noisy like a switchboard, café, quiet like a study); and tried working at different times of day in different spaces (from sundrenched to shady). While I have surprised even myself (I actually liked the standing desk!), the one element of consistency has been sunshine. I have also discovered that different things work at different times of the day on different projects and at different times of the year. Hacking your flow is a journey, not a destination. What does this mean? In other words, don't assume there is only one terminal destination.

I recently asked a group of clients to talk about their optimal workspaces. They were all different. One client preferred to work offline. Another admitted that they did their best work in a public café. Another talked about taking nearly an hour every morning to clear off her desk, put on motivating tunes, focus on her posture, and ensure she had fresh coffee and water in reach. One client confessed that he works best in the middle of the night when he is walking around his house wearing nothing but underwear. The range of preferences and practices was amazingly diverse and in some cases even humorous. What was clear is that most people already knew the conditions under which they work best but not everyone was permitting themselves to accept where and how they work best. This is not a surprise. From a very young age, we are taught that some environments are better for work than others. By the time we reach the work world as adults, these assumptions are firmly entrenched. The challenge is to let go of these assumptions and focus on what really works best for you.

So, take a moment to think about the different places you have worked from in the past few months. What do you like about them? What do you dislike? Some office spaces provide less agility. Most of us have an overly fixed mindset about our workspace. As you are preparing, think about where you might do your best work next.

Ideally, you will experiment and track this over time to discover trends and themes as they vary based on type of work and settings (this is where personal metrics come into play). Try different conference rooms. Maybe take finite projects to the lunchroom off hours or to a coffee shop close by.

Next start envisioning your ideal workspace. What do you need to perform at your best? As a child, I was raised to have a stapler, pens, sharp pencils, scissors, tape (you get the point) out of sight but accessible without moving from my desk. Maybe there are special types of pens you need to sketch designs or maybe you like access to a printer at your desk. In this mobile, technical age, as long as we have our laptop, we are often less tied to location. There is no judgment: The outcome is to know what you need to optimize your work. This is your space and should not be dictated by anyone else's expectations of what an ideal workspace looks like.

As someone who likes to experiment with different locations, I have a small pouch to carry my essentials: nail file, Tylenol, three pens, a chia bar, instant coffee from Starbucks, and the list goes on. The point is that if you're going to work from various locations, you'll need to be properly equipped. I have triplicate chargers for my phone and laptop: one for my home office, one for my work desk and one for my mobile desk. Why waste time packing these up every day or worse yet, risk being without an essential charger?

Optimizing your workspace is also linked to technology. Have you experimented with multiple monitors? When I'm working on a speech I like to have the outline on one screen and slides on another. Of course, if you're working on multiple screens, your mobility may be reduced. If so, ask yourself what is more important: the ability to work anywhere or access to multiple screens? Again, this will likely depend on what type of work you wish to accomplish. The key is to discover what works best for you, even if it's a standing desk in a noisy café.

OPTIMAL WORK TIME

If there is an experiment on productivity, Chris Bailey has run it. In his book *Productivity Project*, Chris Bailey speaks powerfully to the process of observing when you perform at your best. He has found that most people have what he calls a biological prime time. It is that time when it is easiest for you to think deeply. Eventually you will see certain periods of time are best reserved for deep thinking.

Personally, I like to do *deep work* in the mornings. I schedule "taking care of business" or TCB sprints in the afternoon. During these sprints, I'm focused on responding to client/team needs. Early afternoons tend to be less prime time, so I schedule less demanding meetings and catch up on more routine tasks.

Ultimately this is about you knowing what you need based on what is on your plate to deliver. When I need to really write, for example, I like a big chunk of unplugged time where I don't have to interact, shower, cook, or even sleep ... unless I want to.

Other people I know work best in small spurts. Again, discovering your optimal work time, like optimal workspace, is a highly individual endeavor.

OPTIMAL COLLEAGUES

Years ago, Jim Rohn aptly remarked, "You become the average of the five people you spend the most time with." Rohn is right: Who you spend time with matters. The people in our daily lives have a profound influence. By now, you most likely have noticed that being around certain people brings out the best in you and that others have the absolutely opposite effect. No judgment, just great noticing. So, you know what I'm going to stay next—start spending time with healthy, fit people if you want to get in shape, and start spending time with leaders if you want to learn how to lead more effectively. Spend more time with people in flow if you want to experience more flow.

Think about recent heartfelt conversations. When have you felt deeply inspired? Who has challenged you to be better? Life is a two-way street. Knowing whom you want to spend time with is part A. Figuring out how to ignite the best in you, so these people want to spend time with you, too, is part B. The key is that this can always be hacked by being on the donut, preparing thoroughly, and struggling to create a heartfelt or inspiring connection.

I understand that this may sound intimidating, but it is doable, trust me. In 2011, I met (somewhat purposefully) an inspiring woman in Cartagena, Columbia. What could have been a single encounter, I have intentionally nurtured into a deep friendship despite living 2000 miles away. I am consistently looking for ways to add value to our friendship. We schedule phone dates (that are convenient during her commute). We get together at least 1-2 times each year. That one *chance* lunch has opened up countless new friendships, business relationships and contracts for both of us. Why? I've worked intentionally to foster our friendship and create a reciprocal relationship — one that is a two-way street. In short, she is inspiring to me while I am respectful of her time and committed to helping her expand her networks, too.

This brings me to another key point. There is tremendous power in relationships. Emotional energy is vital to our sustainability and our success. Inspiring, intentional interactions can inject massive energy into our lives. Take notice of the people who inspire you to be your best. Who challenges you to the next step? Who is a grounding force? Where do you want to turn for support? Who helps you cultivate more bandwidth? Who drains your energy?

Just like your work environment, the people you choose to bring into your fold play a critical role in whether or not you are able to get on the donut and stay on the donut.

OPTIMAL FOOD

Clearly what you consume and when matters. There are countless bio-hackers who can provide you with limitless hacks to optimize your biology. Again, the key is to start noticing what positions you to be your best.

Simple example: Spring 2015 when I felt 14 months pregnant, I was dreaming of my skinny jeans and bought a Groupon for a juice cleanse. Many months later, I ordered the juices before the Groupon expired. On the last day of the juice cleanse, I was chatting with a girlfriend about my ideas on how to create more flow. She mirrored back the energy and clarity she heard coming through me. I had a little bounce in my step as we hung up. Moments later I realized this was in part the power of flow but even more so the cleanse. While I knew that food was important, it was my first powerful example of just how much what I ate impacted how I operated.

I know—this is where the excuses start to kick in. Maybe you're already thinking, "That's great for you, Camille, but my diet is so bad, I can't see the connection between my food and my productivity." Or you're thinking, "Great, but I'm too exhausted to change my eating..." or "I'm too overextended to figure out what is right for me" or "If it can't be delivered, I don't have time to eat it." Trust me, in my work with busy executives, I've heard every excuse in the book, but I appreciate that they feel very, very real.

What I know is that what I eat does impact how I feel, how I work and my levels of productivity. I now ask myself, "Will this taste better than I will feel for the next two to four hours?" The answer is usually no. I've also come to accept the fact that when it comes to eating, more rules actually help. But don't assume all the rules have to be punitive. You can also have rules that work pleasure and rewards into your diet, too. The goal is to fuel and nourish your body.

Rules are another example of structures that set you up for success. Remember my mantra: It's a decision; it's a discipline. The discipline is designed to make it easier to be successful. But this doesn't mean you can't break the rules from time to time. Strive for moderation. A broken rule doesn't need to mark the end of your commitment to healthy eating.

To create more flow in your diet, know your vices and don't deprive yourself of the occasional treat. As much as possible, reduce the need to use willpower (don't have ice cream in the house if it's too tempting), and focus as much on adding new and energizing foods as on eliminating those foods that just drag you down.

TRIGGERS

In Chapter 3 we explored the concept of triggers. There are certain conditions, situations or experiences that impact us in profoundly different ways. For whatever reason, some stimuli can trigger us to step up, be magnificent and other stimuli can reduce us to a mess. When we feel triggered, the result can be intense. Sometimes we are triggered so fast, we are not sure exactly what has happened.

By better understanding which triggers accelerate our capacity to experience flow, we can re-think and redesign a more compelling, inspiring, flow-filled existence that optimizes while minimizing drain.

We know behavioral change is hard: Understanding and harnessing our triggers is one way to make it easier. Being disciplined to hack our triggers can provide both joy and significant self-control. Expert coach Marshall Goldsmith captures this masterfully in his book *Triggers: Creating the Behavior that Lasts*. Goldsmith's argument is simple: Harnessing triggers is the practice of deliberately designing environmental cues that inspire your best. The key is not perfection, but rather to move you consistently, rigorously towards being your very best. In a simple but powerful example, Goldsmith answers the same 22 questions each and every night to a friend. Each question starts with, "Did I do my best..." The specifics might change based on work priorities, but the practice is consistent. Even more impressive, each night he gives himself a score on 1–10 for each item! Goldsmith built a system for measuring what matters most, and as a result, he is doing a better job managing it.

Of course, triggers come in many shapes and sizes. Like most things in life, there are often two sides to each situation: the sunny and cloudy. Regardless of whether triggers bring out the best or worst in you, we want to capture and think them through. The key is to notice our triggers, name them and hack them, so that we can turn them into things that are working for rather than against us!

For example, I once had a client who felt like he was never living up to his full potential. As we worked together, a few things became clear. First, he was virtually oblivious to positive triggers. Turns out he was most productive late at night but felt like he should be most productive at 5:00 am, because he had grown up in a family where early mornings were valued as a work time. This was not his biological prime time, but he was stubbornly ignoring this fact. Second, he was convinced he did his best work at the office. Turns out he was most productive when he was hiding out at his favorite café far away from the immediate demands of his "official" workspace. As we worked together, he identified these positive triggers and started to honor them. We also started to explore his negative triggers. For example, he knew that seeing his brother was always emotionally draining, but he had difficulty saying no, even when on a deadline. Over time he started to recognize these meetings as a negative trigger and to find ways to schedule meetings with his brother during periods when his work demands were low.

Of course, flow hacking doesn't need to be so serious or all about work. In fact, the more we start to understand our triggers, the more we are able to *gamify* the process. Understanding and hacking the triggers that optimize our productivity can be vast and range from the mundane (e.g., what you eat or when you sleep) to the profound (e.g., harnessing the power of why and your deeper calling to impact our world). They can be internal (e.g., your mindset) or external (e.g., your work environment). What matters is that when you know your triggers, you are better able to accelerate the execution of an important project.

FEEDBACK

In earlier chapters, we explored the importance of creating clear outcomes and metrics. Here we dive deeper. Feedback is a vital flow trigger. When we have the right metrics, we get real time, regular feedback, and thus are better able to control flow! Why? As humans, we feel happiness or satisfaction not from accomplishing a project but rather from being able to see noticeable progress. The key is to identify what is important and then to create easily accessible metrics to track how you are coming along.

Once again, there are many experts who have focused on how to create and use metrics. There is an entire movement now that aims to quantify the self by identifying what is important and implementing metrics to measure these factors. Examples range from the very simple, such as a calorie-counting app for recording food points, to more complex heart monitors. As we increasingly move into the field of big data, doing this is becoming both easier and harder. Yes, there are now more tools than ever before to track data. The process keeps getting harder, however, because now it can be difficult to assess what really matters and to make sure we are prioritizing the right kinds of data to achieve our desired outcomes.

Simple example: Several years ago, I volunteered to beta-test a product focused on optimizing maternal health. With my advanced maternal age (I was a dinosaur in fertility years), I was a rare find. They gave me numerous gadgets to check different metrics: Fitbit to measure activity, scale to track weight gain, a blood pressure cuff that plugged into an iPhone to track blood pressure, software to track food, caffeine, water and the list goes on. While the scale provided valuable data, and was a much-needed upgrade, it was the Fitbit that transformed my existence far beyond pregnancy. Getting real time, quantifiable data on my activity (or lack thereof) is highly rewarding and motivating.

Years ago, Ray Fowler, the CEO of the American Psychological Association, committed to getting healthy. He adopted an old-school pedometer and was diligent. He shed lots of weight, moved from walking to running, and eventually ran marathons. To see him today, he is the picture of health. Why? Because like my former client, he realized that what gets measured gets managed and what gets managed gets done! My point is simple: Part of the journey is using metrics to clarify outcomes because once again, without clear outcomes, arriving at the destination is next to impossible. But this brings us to the next challenge: continuously tapping into valuable feedback.

HARNESS THE POWER OF FEEDBACK

Most often we feel happiest when we see that we are making progress towards things that are important. Feedback is vital to seeing progress. Ultimately, feedback is an opportunity to get perspective, calibrate and adjust to be more impactful.

CULTIVATE INTERNAL AND EXTERNAL FEEDBACK

Ideally, all organizations would create cultures where everyone is expected to build their capacity to step back, get perspective and provide analytical feedback. All too often we default the responsibility of giving feedback to others. The most consistent and reliable source of feedback is you. Why? It is completely inside your circle of control to prioritize developing the ability to give this feedback to yourself. This requires three things: a supportive environment, time to reflect, and a culture that promotes self-awareness. Again, remember that feedback is a vital trigger to peak performance.

Time and again, I have found the most powerful gateway to behavior changes is positive feedback. Spend any time with our 3-year-old son, and you will be painfully reminded of this reality. And yet, all too often we overlook this. Think about potty training or learning to ride a bike: Very few of us were 100% successful the first time we tried but the adults celebrated our small steps forward anyway.

Research shows that we need three positive comments to counterbalance one negative comment. Unfortunately, as a culture, we are not setting ourselves up for success because we tend to give 10 negative comments for every positive comment.

Too often we have an erroneously fixed mindset that giving feedback has to be negative, painful and happen during a review. Start to notice how profoundly impactful feedback is as a trigger for flow, and hopefully you will get on the donut and be more purposeful with feedback to yourself and to those around you.

GIVE FEEDBACK IN REAL TIME

Effective feedback is timely, frequent and linked directly to actions. The more concrete and actionable the feedback, the quicker individuals will be able to integrate, adapt and respond to situations in an impactful manner. Now consider the typical annual review where individuals receive general scores that are sums of all their actions over the past year. These reviews fail because the feedback is all too often devoid of context and disconnected from the work it seeks to evaluate. On the contrary, when I was working on this book, I engaged an editor to work with me in real time. Receiving immediate feedback helped me hack small problems before they turned into major obstacles. As a result, I was able to stay on schedule and meet my goal.

RETHINK THE "REVIEWER"

Traditionally, feedback has been a top-down experience. In reality, most valuable, relevant and accurate feedback comes from those people who see you in action the most—typically this is your peers or your team.

Regardless of your position, you can shift the culture of feedback. Simply start to give everyone around you, and I mean everyone, positive feedback on the things you see them doing right. Praise anything that you notice creating a positive ripple. Do this religiously, and you will feel the greatest ripple. Why? You are building a mindset to see goodness. You will cultivate your skills to give feedback and the more time you spend giving feedback, regardless of the type, the better you will get feedback, too. Of course, for this loop to work, the feedback must be genuine, specific and heartfelt. People intuitively know when you are blowing smoke. We like people less if they are disingenuous than if they say nothing at all.

GET MORE

While feedback is vital to flow, we spend far too little time proactively seeking it out. The flow cycle also applies to getting feedback. Think about the people who provide you the most valuable, impactful feedback. What is it about them and your relationship with them that attracts you? How do they share feedback that makes it valuable and actionable? Can you get more feedback from them more often? How might you make clear requests for feedback to colleagues? Is there a way to make feedback more valuable and relevant? Have you intentionally thought through and invited people to give you feedback?

When it came to marriage, I was a very late bloomer. Maybe it was having mediated the divorce of so many couples in grad school or maybe it was that I simply hadn't met my metaphoric lobster yet. By my late 30s, I had a closet full of bridesmaids' dresses. And, twice, as part of the bridal party, I had expressed concerns about the bride's choice of life partner. I'm of the belief that standing in someone's wedding is a commitment to stand beside the couple throughout their marriage. If I'm not convinced the marriage is a good one, I feel a moral obligation to have that conversation. And yes, once I was uninvited from the bridal party. Both times these brides came to appreciate my courage. One divorced within a year (I'm glad I didn't buy an ugly dress for that one!) and to this day, her family credits me for having the courage to have a conversation they were too cowardly to have. Sadly, the other committed suicide leaving behind a complicated, sad gaggle of kids. In my thirties, I identified three people from different stages of life with different experiences and proactively asked them to give me feedback on my choice of partner. All three gave the thumbs up, were at my wedding, and continue on as dear friends. What matters is that you think about whose feedback you appreciate and actively cultivate ways to engage in feedback to accelerate yourself and your goals.

FEEDBACK PITFALLS

This brings us to feedback pitfalls. First, just because you don't like the feedback, don't hate the reviewer! Instead, notice your reactions. Are you quick to dismiss something? What makes you most uncomfortable? Noticing these responses (sometimes triggers) creates opportunities for learning, progress and potential hacking. Moreover, when you receive "tough" feedback, step back and think. Who is giving it, what resonates and what doesn't? You have choices. You don't have to like everything you hear. You don't even have to accept it. You simply have to cultivate the ability to take in everything, absorb and digest it, and then decide what to use. Finally, notice if you reject all negative feedback or accept all positive feedback. If you're too one sided, it might be time to revisit your mindset.

FIND YOUR FAILURES

We are a culture that craves innovation and yet actively resists failing. Innovation by definition is about trying new and different approaches, which means that failure is part of the package. By actively looking for our failures, we can unleash new potential.

Entrepreneurs know that failing, sometimes often, is critical to eventually being successful. And investors at all levels know that the best investments they make are with people who learn constantly. Ask any experienced entrepreneur and they will share that to be experienced is to have tried and failed. What makes these entrepreneurs experienced is their tenacity, mindset, and commitment to learning from everything they do, even investments they may want to forget.

I believe cultivating a find-your-failures culture is vital to creating more flow and to quality living. It is about failing forward, so that we are always learning and growing. In contrast, a fixed mindset is deeply threatened by finding fails. For those people, it is not safe to fail and definitely not safe to share fails with others.

By sharing fails, we live a growth mindset. Sharing actively cultivates learning, humility, and connection. The simple act of sharing your fails ensures that others won't make the same mistakes, inspires others to take risks themselves and positions you to learn from their fumbles.

I have one client who has been on *Inc*'s fastest growing company for five years running. They actively live with an internal company mantra, "Make it bad, make it better." The key is that they are always in action and always improving. With anything new, you have to do it once for the first time to be able to hack it and make it better. Said differently, the only true fail is paralysis.

Cultivating a mindset to find your fails means that we are reflecting on and reviewing our own work. What worked? What could have worked better? The more we reframe fails to be a learning victory and celebrate finding a fail means the more likely we will learn and grow. By analyzing what we did and where there are opportunities to improve, we reveal learning and growth that might not otherwise be apparent.

Sometimes there are massive fails (e.g., losing a core client) and other times there are minor fails (e.g. leaving behind a diaper bag). Either way, the goal is to find ways to hack these fails so that they don't happen again. The mindset requires intention and attention: It is a decision and a discipline. Again, it requires grit to examine oneself with rigor and always stay in the learning zone.

For example, let's say you allocate 30 minutes to struggle hard on a project. If you fail to move forward, you can look back on the challenge to understand what tasks were poorly assigned. Did you not break them into small enough pieces? Was there not the right level of tensions? Did you not have the right resources (knowledge, team member, time, attention) for the task at hand? Maybe you did not think through the environment thoroughly and were distracted. Cultivating a mindset that proactively looks for and finds fails is vital to the hacking mindset. And yes, it is a lifelong journey!

FAILS HAPPEN: HERE'S HOW YOU CAN MAXIMIZE THE LEARNING

Last summer I had a massive medical fail. It happens. I failed to put the required time and energy into preparation for a medical procedure and luckily, I dodged a potentially life-changing bullet. Having both a maternal and a paternal uncle suffering from colon cancer, I went in for a proactive colonoscopy five years early.

There is nothing fun about prepping for a colonoscopy. I had hosted my uncle in my home prior to two colon surgery preps and had far too much experience with the process. Walking out the door the morning of my colonoscopy, I thought to myself, "The worst is over. Everybody says the prep is the worst part." And yet, somehow, I knew it wasn't.

Although I had specifically asked the technician for enough medication to go to "lala land," I woke up feeling like I was actively wrestling with the technician. I was uncomfortable — really uncomfortable. In the recovery room, they told me the discomfort was just gas.

My husband brought me from the procedure to the hospital where I was supposed to meet with my uncle's surgical team. About 10 minutes into the meeting I left, doubled over in pain and unable to track the conversation. At home I tried to sleep it off but lay in bed moaning. I called a dear doctor friend and explained the situation and described my torturous abdominal pain. I asked her if I should go to the ER. In the end, we waited hours for an x-ray. Then we waited for it to be read. Then we waited for a CAT scan, and later, we waited for the CAT scan to be read.

Several hours later a surgical resident was briefing me on my situation. I needed surgery to remove 7 inches of my colon where there was a tear. There is a risk that I would end up with an ileostomy (put bluntly, this is a pouch to poop into).

I texted a dear neighbor friend, "In the ER, prepping for surgery, botched colonoscopy. Can you spend night/watch my kids?" I texted another dear doctor friend: "In ER, prepping for surgery from botched colonoscopy. I know there are questions I should be asking...time for call? Here's my patient ID #."

Within minutes one friend was *en route* to my home and the other had pulled up my record, was on the phone, and was asking great questions of the surgical resident: "Had she seen the report of the polyps they had removed from my colon? Did she know the location of the tear? Did she know the type of removal process?" To my credit, I knew there were important questions to ask, I just wasn't trained to know what they were.

About this time, my first doctor friend showed up in the ER. The situation was significant enough that she wanted to be there to ask the doctors questions and serve as a support. The chief surgical resident was taken aback by my personal medical team .... so much so that the surgeon decided to wake up the chief radiologist to read the CAT scan. The chief radiologist noted that the tears were on the back not front, which is apparently an important distinction, and suggested that we wait it out through the night to see if my conditions became more complicated or not. This turned out to be a sage decision and soon I was on the mend. What did I learn?

First, friendships really matter. There is no price for having friends to whom you can send one text message and know that your kids will be covered as long as you need them to be. In this day and age, having doctor friends is really important. Invest in friendships and give proactively; you never know when you will need to call up your friends for support and advice. Second, I learned to ask good questions. I didn't know what questions to ask the surgical residents, but I did know how to find the right people to ask the right questions. Master the capacity to ask good questions or have friends around who can ask them on your behalf.

Finally, get a colonoscopy! My intuition was right. I was at risk. I had four polyps removed, three of which were precancerous. It is really important to do this proactive test and be proactive in your health care generally. It is also really important that you research who is doing the colonoscopy before you go in.

To be clear, I'm retelling this story here because it was a huge fail on my part. I failed to prepare, and I paid a price for my lack of preparation. But I also learned from this fail, and learning from fails is ultimately also essential to flow.

EXPECTATION SETTING

By now you have a long list of different things you can do to optimize your ability for flow. But remember, trying to do everything is a recipe for doing nothing. As I have said throughout this book, get clear on the outcome while staying flexible on the approach! This has been our mantra from Chapter 1 and for a good reason. After all, we need to make sure that we know what is important and are setting clear, realistic, actionable expectations for ourselves, but leave plenty of room for different avenues to get there.

One of the most valuable gifts you can give yourself is to execute on at least some of the activities or sustained practices I have discussed so far. As you have already seen, this doesn't need to be drastic. At its best, tapping into flow is a process of gently, consistently peeling the layers of the onion. If you haven't already started, don't worry—there is still time.

In fact, by the time you finish this book, you will already have a deeper understanding, and it will hopefully be that much easier to get started. What matters most? First, it is vital to fully prepare, prioritize and optimize tasks. Second, it is vital to drill down on outcomes. Finally, it is time to jump into purposeful struggle. Throughout the process, bear in mind that there is a fine line between optimism and realism. In the final chapter, I explore just a few success strategies to help you launch into flow.

SUMMARY

Hack everything you can to get into flow! Hack your workspace, your time, your colleagues and your diet. Hack whatever you need to hack to move the dial forward. While you're hacking, don't forget to also:

Know your triggers: Find out what makes you work at your best and what drags you down. Amplify positive triggers and eliminate the negative ones.

Get feedback: Seek it out! Without feedback, you risk stagnation.

Find your fails: Appreciate that you have to fail to grow.

Set expectations: Have clear expectations. Without these, you will have no clear destination or outcome to work toward.

8

SUCCESS STRATEGIES

Changing how you think and engage with your work and life takes time. If you've always ignored or tried to avoid fails, paying attention to fails when they happen — and recognizing that they can actually help you — is going to take a bit of work. It means developing new habits. More importantly, it means changing your perspective on fails — seeing them as an opportunity for change rather than an embarrassment. Likewise, if you're someone who has long ignored your triggers — both positive and negative — it might take a few weeks or months to become deeply attuned to your triggers and start harnessing their energy to get on the donut and stay there. This is precisely why I want to leave you with just a few more strategies for success.

OPTIMIZE YOU

Flow hacking is designed to help you understand yourself even more deeply. Self-understanding is the gateway to optimizing what we do so we can perform at our very best more often.

If you have been contemplating this book's call to action as you are reading, you are likely already close to developing your own personal "Optimization Manual" (unfortunately, we get owner's manuals for most things that are important but never receive nor take time to create one for ourselves!). When we are truly optimized, however, we can take it another step forward by developing our very own owner's manual. Keeping track of personal successes and failures helps us to know how to rev up, tune in, stay focused, and troubleshoot our own glitches. Tim Ferriss, a legendary biohacker, keeps copious journals of his different experiments so that he can track which actions created which states (and recreate them as desired). Like Ferriss, we should all be charting our progress.

LIVE PURPOSEFULLY

This is a big topic and the focus of many books. We believe that certain structures (habits, systems and strategies) contribute to feeling more fulfilled more often. Finding your life purpose can take hard work. Developing strategies to live purposefully (on the donut or in the learning zone) make this pursuit easier.

The outcome is not that you live my purposeful lifestyle, of course, but rather that you identify what works for you. To begin, experiment by creating daily, weekly, and monthly check-in points. While each of these has different levels of scrutiny, the key is building into your life the time and the skills required to get perspective. The outcome is realizing what you need to be your best and to more effectively cultivate agility under any circumstance.

SUCCESS LEAVES CLUES. FIND THEM!

Rarely does success happen by chance alone. People who are consistently successful have consistently built strategies that work for them. The more time you spend with people who are successful, the more exposure you have to their habits and the more likely you will be able to identify and then replicate them.

This means that if you want to find clues to success, surround yourself with successful people. Identify those people in your circle, whether you know them closely or not, and start to observe their success strategies. Yes, I'm telling you to copy everything you might think is contributing to their success! Fortunately, people invariably like to talk about themselves. What does this mean for you? Develop a list of killer questions, build rapport with these people you admire, and then engage them in order to uncover what it is that makes them successful.

SOLVING FOR STRESS

Throughout this book, we have talked about different strategies to hack challenges with the goal of injecting the right amount of tension to optimize performance without compromising our well-being. Living in the learning zone is about stretching ourselves to build capacity without building too much stress. But even with the most persistent commitment to health and hacking, stress happens. There are inevitable bumps in the road, unexpected challenges and, as I confessed in the previous chapter, even botched colonoscopies. Living with a hacking mindset, we notice those situations and find periods of calm, after the fact, to reflect and identify stressors. Maybe there are skills that can help you prevent future occurrences of stress? Living with a hacking mindset is about consciously and consistently putting yourself back into the driver's seat.

HACKING SUCCESS
IN A SUSTAINABLE MANNER

This brings us to one of the most important takeaways this book has to offer — hack everything! Disrupt your assumptions about the "right" way to do something. Focus on the desired result and then get creative, flexible and disruptive in how you achieve the result. As I've said, be clear on the outcome, and flexible on the approach.

Here is just a shortlist of some of my favorite hacks, but once again, your own list may look a bit different. Some hacks are universal and others are very individual. What matters most is developing a list of hacks that work for you wherever you go.

Establish morning rituals: Whether you're an early morning riser or someone who likes to sleep in and start working after the morning rush hour, identify the very best morning rituals for you. These will be personal but should at the very least involve carving out time to fuel up for the day in mind, body, and spirit (yes, nourish your body with more than coffee). Think about what you need to do to make it a great day; collate your to-dos to create more time and bandwidth; and establish one or two major priorities for the day. If you have a plan, you'll be more likely to spend the day on the donut and in flow rather than simply taking things as they come.

Eat salad for breakfast: We all know about daily nutritional recommendations for fruits and vegetables. If you can't find time to eat vegetables for lunch, try starting your day with a salad instead! Most people have more control over what they eat for breakfast than other meals. Use these moments to lay the foundations of good nutrition. Most people have lots of assumptions or conditioning about what they should eat for breakfast, but there is nothing stopping us from swapping carbs for kale.

Focus on nutrition: In our fast-paced world there are thousands of moving parts. Although we know the importance of what we eat, it can at times be an easy ball to drop. Fortunately, there are limitless hacks to address this problem. To begin, try weekend food preparation for the entire week and keep healthy snacks accessible. I jokingly call sweet bell peppers a "road sandwich." Again, challenge your assumptions and explore eating a pepper like you might eat an apple. They are sweet, crunchy, nutritious, and low in calories.

Exercise as a family activity: Carving time for exercise is hard for everyone. If you have small children and less time to go to the gym, find ways to make exercise a family affair. Buy a jogging stroller and bring your kids along for the run. During the winter months, we often take our kids with us to the gym. Identify small snippets of time for exercise. It is amazing how many weights you can lift in 15 minute sprints. My fall back is burpees. They are intense squat thrusts and something you can do anywhere from the boardroom to the bedroom to an airport lounge.

Know your values: Time and again I have worked with individuals and organizations to clarify their values. Why is this vital to hacking flow? Invariably there are bumps along the road when we are forced to make difficult choices. If we have thought pro-actively about our values, it becomes much easier to move forward in the face of adversity. Ask yourself: What matters to you? Prioritize your values. Keep them in a visible place. Return to them when you are in doubt.

Hack home sore spots: We all have those places in our home that gather "stuff." Notice where your dumping grounds are and hack options for cleaning up. One participant does a 10-minute tidy every night where she runs around to see how much she can get done in a short period of time. I have adopted my daughter's wagon to load up things that don't belong in a given room. One wagon ride can get the right things to the right room! If you haven't already done so, read Marie Kondo's *The Life-Changing Magic of Tidying Up.* Less is always more.

Build strong partnerships: There is power in being a part of a team whether at work, at home, at the gym or in your service work. But great partnerships are typically the result of intentional effort. The more honest we are and the more curious we are, the more we will gain from entering into partnerships and the more sustainable they will be.

But great partnerships take work. They require ground rules, and even a secret language. My husband and I have cultivated a whole underground language to give each other feedback in ways that won't lead to a fight. We have weekly team meetings. When things go wrong, and they always do, we spend time talking it out and identifying alternatives. The point is that we don't take our marriage for granted; that's how our partnership stays solid.

Make real asks: We all want to feel valued and needed. Assuming you have invested in relationships over time, you can make these more real by sharing your needs and asking for help. To do this well, we must be aware of and share our needs. When I was launching my CreateMoreFlow site, I invited friends and colleagues to beta test the content for free. I was adding value by sharing the content and new ideas. I asked each person who participated to give candid, real-time feedback to make the content even better. Think about what you need to move forward. Think about what you can realistically ask for from your friends who are also likely already stretched by friends and family. Be true to yourself about what types of support you require to excel.

Create financial ownership: Cultivating responsibility and a sense of ownership is important to flow hacking. This can be challenging. Over lunch at a recent conference where I was giving a keynote, the discussion turned to 529 plans and saving money for our children's college years. My husband and I started saving for our 1- and 3-year-old kids and are acutely aware that funding a college education can have a double edge. After sitting with the question of whether traditional colleges will actually be relevant to kids in 15 to 20 years, the conversation shifted. How do you engage kids so that they understand and truly value the resources that we are saving to invest in them?

After throwing around a few ideas, one mother shared what I thought was a brilliant hack. Each semester her college-bound children take out a loan for their tuition, books, room-and-board, and so on. They have a very clear, very specific contracting conversation about what their expectations are (e.g., attending class, taking quality notes, studying, and reaching certain grade benchmarks). They discuss strategies for identifying hard classes, for seeking additional help and for modulating peer pressure. By the end, this mother and her kids are crystal clear on expectations and consequences. If these expectations are met, the parents pay the loan in full. If these expectations are not met, the child-student owns the loan. It's a simple and brilliant example of building in accountability by establishing clear expectations and outcomes.

Automate: By now you most likely have noticed those things that need to happen and hopefully you are hacking the recurring tasks. Whether it is the practice of swapping out seasonal clothes in your closet, preparing for birthdays or ensuring that you have the right tires on your vehicle for the right season, there is lots of life that needs to happen. Unmanaged, it can interrupt your ability to be purposeful in the moment. One strategy is to notice when you need something and build a system to capture it so that it can be automated. Once you start doing this, your life will slowly but surely become less distracted by attending to needs, whether they are weekly or annual needs. Here's a simple example: I live in New England and have made a habit of putting on snow tires by Thanksgiving weekend. I have a recurring calendar reminder for 11/1 to make the annual appointment for the tires to be changed. Simply put, I'm never that working mom who suddenly has to drop everything to deal with a snowstorm, at least not the snow tires aspect. Also on 11/1, I capture all the great Halloween costumes that I saw the night before to seed ideas for the coming year.

Read/screen with purpose: There are thousands of great resources available on the web. The challenge is tracking what you want to read and having it available when you want it. I'm a raving fan of the apps Instapaper and Pocket. I encounter great, relevant resources every day. Instapaper allows me to collate them and read them on my time (not when I see them). Similarly, there are great things to be watched. Cultivating a habit to know what you want to watch saves time. I use Wunderlist to have ever-ready hyperlinks to Ted talks and great movies.

Scrapbook 2.0: As much as I love looking at the baby book my mother lovingly made for me, I know that I won't do that for my kids. Instead, I created a Gmail account for each of my children. Although they can't read yet, I send them emails with fun anecdotes and pictures of our adventures. Some day they will be able to access all these memories — in the cloud. Call it scrapbooking in the digital age!

Get promoted: Hacks can be small (e.g., digitizing your child's baby book) but they can also be big (e.g., getting promoted at work). So how do you hack something as significant as a promotion? If you want to be promoted, you have to plan proactively and participate. All too often we "keep our head down," do great work and expect our work to be recognized, rewarded, and reinforced. But getting a promotion isn't really about magic. To get promoted you need to gather your facts, build a fan base, leverage your connections, and plan. Invariably success leaves clues. Engage someone who has been promoted to review what works. And if you're in flow, promotions will be more easily obtained for one simple reason. Flow begets more flow. Flow is infectious. You are more productive and creative in flow. When you're in flow, people are simply more likely to want to be around you and keep you around for the long term, too.

SUMMARY

Your strategies for success will not be exactly the same as my strategies for success, and they shouldn't be. We all have different triggers. We all have different goals. We all thrive under different conditions. My hot tub may be your favorite local café. My morning salad may be your homemade granola. You get the point! You are free to take or leave the specifics. What matters is continually exploring what makes you even better, and embracing these conditions to get into flow more often. Specifically, this means honing in on a few key points: _

> **Discover how to optimize you:** Develop a personal user's manual (you're the only person who can do this) about what positions you to be your very best and use this manual to take better care of yourself.

> **Live purposefully:** Know thyself and know thy purpose.

> **Find the clues to success:** Look at your own successes and the successes of those around you and gather the clues to build momentum.

> **Solve for stress:** Pay attention to your pressure points. When does pressure feed you and when does it start breaking you down? Know your breaking point to avoid spending too much time beyond terror's very outer edge.

> **Hack for success:** Hack everything you can: what you eat, where you work, who is on your team, how you run your daily life, when and how often you let go and the list goes on. Leave nothing untouched!

AFTERWORD

Guess what? I wrote the first draft of this book in five and a half days. Perhaps even more remarkable is the fact that I wrote the first draft of this book during the final two weeks of 2016 — a time of year when many people are buckling under the weight of end-of-year financial commitments and personal obligations. Better yet, I managed to do this close to home and work, for minimal expense and without escaping to an off-the-grid cabin in the woods or returning to Sedona where I wrote my first book. In fact, I never left the Boston area and even squeezed in a few days to celebrate and reconnect with family and friends. How did I do it all? I did it by putting everything I write about in this book into action.

CLEAR ON THE OUTCOME, FLEXIBLE ON THE APPROACH

I am passionate about creating more flow and have seen how it has transformed my life and the lives of my clients and friends. I knew that I needed to write a new book on how to create more flow and to share these ideas with a wider audience. I started to explore the idea for the book in Fall 2016. My earliest commitment was to turn out the book by mid-November. I realized that I needed a chunk of focused, uninterrupted time to think deeply, but, given my commitments to my clients, that didn't work out. I was swamped with speaking engagements, client meetings, and the everyday demands of life itself.

Because I was already clear on the outcome and flexible on the approach, I simply took this as a sign that I needed to reschedule the project. Unlike some of my friends and colleagues who can write in very short spurts (just 20 to 30 minutes per day), I knew that I was the kind of writer who needed a bigger chunk of time to tackle the project. I also realized the best time to do this would be right before and during the holidays in December (it is a typically quiet time for me as my clients are focused on the holidays).

Take Away: Sometimes you will have a clear goal but need to adjust the timeline for achieving it. If this is the case, don't beat yourself up. The ability to identify the optimal time to work on a major project is an essential skill. While it is true that some delays are pure procrastination, often delays are a critical intervention.

PREPARATION

All through the final quarter of the year I was preparing for the book. When I had a writing engagement — for example, an article for *Forbes*—I would focus on writing about flow in order to help create an archive of related materials for the book. This also furthered my thinking.

When I had a speaking engagement, I would be certain to save any relevant notes for the book. When I was running, I would stop to record critical thoughts about the book. The book was in the back of my mind for months and even though I wasn't actively working on it, I was accumulating an archive of materials for the project. When I sat down to write, a lot of the work, including much of the critical thinking, had already been done. Most importantly, I had no doubt in my mind that I needed to write the book — it was timely and essential.

Take Away: Preparation takes time, but you can prepare for future projects while engaged in your daily work. The more synergy there is in everything you do, the more likely it is that preparation for future projects will happen as a matter of course. When this occurs, you also reduce your reliance on willpower.

CREATE OPTIMAL CONDITIONS

I knew that in order to execute this challenge in a short timeframe (two weeks), I would need to create the optimal conditions under which to write.

With two small children at home, writing into the wee hours of the evening (even if I'm in flow) isn't an option. If you write until 3:00 am and then have a small person wake you up at 6:00 am, you're not likely to be able to sustain your writing practice. Writing during the day at the office or at home is also less than ideal. When you have people in your life with an attention span that stretches for minutes (sometimes seconds), not hours, sustaining longer projects can be challenging. I also knew from the experience of writing my first book that I write best when I step out of my everyday life. And as noted earlier in the book, I also knew that I write best when I have access to a hot tub! So, this is precisely what I arranged to do.

I took four days the week before Christmas to step out of my regular life—just for four days. My husband is also a working professional with lots of demands, and four days is what we could manage. I knew that a retreat in the desert wasn't in the cards (I didn't want to spend precious time on a flight!), so I went to work on the book at a friend's home 20 minutes away. It was a mutually beneficial exchange: They were out of town and needed a cat sitter. And yes, they also have a hot tub!

With these optimal conditions in place, I started to push forward. Of course, surprises do happen. While working on the book I was hit with a nasty head cold and even nastier stomach bug (a tough combo) which slowed me down, but did not stop me from working. On the home front, my husband reported an even worse nasty stomach virus had arrived, leaving my husband and children down for a few days. Committed to pushing my book forward, I kept working through the cold and with the help of a friend, sent a bit of backup in to my home. In the end, the misfortunes of my husband and children had one silver lining. My husband suggested I stay away until everyone was feeling better.

Take Away: Work and life are connected and to achieve a healthy work-life integration, at times we need to do more than compartmentalize. We need to optimize. This means taking a good, long look at everything from our work space to our home and ensuring it is all running as smoothly as possible. It was far easier to step away for an intensive writing period than to fight for those moments. For my next book, I will schedule away time to focus on the revisions as well. But again, this is all part of learning from my fails.

ASSEMBLE A GREAT TEAM

Don't kid yourself. Everything is easier with the right people. Even solitary activities like writing require a team. As suggested above, my husband was a critical part of this team. He agreed to take on my share of the childcare and domestic work for several days in order to buy me time to work on this book. The friend who came to the rescue with additional supplies when my family was down was also on the team. Back in the office, my assistant was fielding calls and managing clients.

And online, I was working with an editor who gave me ongoing feedback on every chapter as it was completed. This was vital. Having someone available for an immediate read and edit enabled me to keep moving forward. Being able to call her when I was stuck — really stuck — was profound. I craved feedback and recognize that is a critical part of how I sustain momentum and flow. While I still had to write the book, having a team in place was essential, too. Although we work together seamlessly, I have never met my editor nor my assistant in person.

Take Away: Grit and the right mindset alone are rarely enough to achieve outstanding outcomes. Whatever your strengths, assemble a supportive, complementary team.

CREATE MORE
BANDWIDTH AND MORE TIME

By creating optimal conditions (writing at a friend's house for a few days) and downloading some tasks (asking my assistant to manage clients or asking my editor to give immediate and meaningful feedback when I got stuck on a chapter), I did two essential things that made it possible to write this book. First, I cleared the deck, so to speak, and created more bandwidth (mental, emotional and physical) to focus on the task at hand. Second, I created more time in order to actually complete the task. Having two finite periods of time (four days before Christmas and one and a half after the holiday) created significant tension to keep pushing forward, and a period of three days in between sprints to be with family, to rest up, and to recharge. I knew that I could manage that intensity for short sprints. Especially in a quiet, clean, space of solitude.

Take Away: Identify what you need to be successful. Challenge assumptions about how you will get things done. Clear the decks and create more bandwidth. When you lack bandwidth, you aren't working at your full capacity.

HACK THE PROCESS

In many respects this book is the result of effective hacking. Before I abandoned my family for four days of writing, I filled the fridge with healthy foods (which they didn't end up eating because of the bug). I also cleared the "to-do list" and finished our holiday shopping online. I also checked my own packing list to ensure that I would show up at my friends' house with everything I needed to survive (chocolate, coffee, eggnog, a swimsuit and butt glue). I didn't want to be running home to retrieve books, clothes or a toothbrush in the middle of my short, nearby writing retreat.

I also hacked the writing process itself. A dear friend and professional writer, Joanne Gordon Berk, mentored me in the process of organizing my thoughts. My first book, *Rewired*, was quick to write but then took well over a year to edit and organize. Based on Jo's coaching, I had captured hundreds of thoughts, notes, blog posts, and ideas onto individual index cards. I sorted the index cards into piles (beginning, middle, end). I then sorted each pile into chapters and subsections. Part of the process was getting ideas out of my head and onto paper. Invariably, like the Create More Time hack, the more I emptied ideas onto paper, the more space there was for new, different and at times better ideas. Part of the process was organizing the ideas. Physically moving the cards was a powerful way to focus on how ideas could be presented. It also meant that when I went to sit down and write, I had already been thinking through organization.

I then assembled eighteen months of writing and previously published articles—all my materials on flow—and put them into a single document. By the time I started, I already had a well-established starting place.

Take Away: Don't reinvent the wheel. You probably already know what works and what doesn't work. Exploit this expertise.

STEP BACK AND GET PERSPECTIVE

Remember my comments earlier about the need to step off the dance floor from time-to-time and get perspective from, let's say, the balcony? On December 30, one day before my personal deadline, I finished a first draft of the book. This is when I stepped back, and I really do mean stepped back. I put the document in Google Docs and shared it with my husband, friends, and some trusted clients. I stepped back to reflect on the process while others started to read and leave comments. Two weeks later I had a better sense of where the book was already on fire and where it needed more work. During those two weeks, I got back to working on some of the things I had sidelined in the last two weeks of the year while sprinting on the book. This type of perspective is vital to rethink what really matters, what is good enough, and where I have lost track of my ideas, as well as what I should hone further.

Take Away: Don't be afraid to step off the dance floor. Sometimes it can be really hard to not be moving forward on a project you feel is important, and sometimes this space is vital to optimize your capacity to move forward. Use this time to survey what you have already accomplished, or to return to work previously sidelined. Value the time you spend on the sidelines. After all, it is essential to flow, too.

REWARD YOURSELF AND KEEP LEARNING

When the book was done, I rewarded myself. I already admitted in the preface that writing is not something that I find easy. It has always been a bit of struggle, even though I see myself as a writer; it's an integral part of my identity and work. So, when I finished the book, I let myself bask in the thought that I had in fact done it! I celebrated with family and friends. I also took time out to jot down what did and did not work about the process. Did I prepare enough? Did I create enough bandwidth and time, or did I need a bit more room? How did I handle unexpected obstacles along the way? In short, what would I replicate and what would I change next time around?

Take Away: Celebrate your accomplishments. Let yourself take time out to feel proud of what you have already done. Also, take stock of what helped you arrive at your desired outcome. This will make achieving things in the future even easier.

CONCLUDING THOUGHTS

When I turn my attention to my next big project, I can say with confidence that I will have an even more sharply honed plan on how to get into flow and stay in flow for the duration of the project. And that is what makes creating more flow ultimately so amazing. Flow begets more flow. Why? Because part of creating more flow is about constantly stepping back to observe the process — what is working (what is keeping you afloat and in flow) and what is not working (what is dragging you down). In other words, being in flow not only feels great and heightens your productivity, but it also helps you understand how to be in flow more often. And this brings me to my parting thoughts.

When we turn our attention to flow we are not going off the grid and eliminating all technology. In fact, as I have emphasized throughout this book, we can even use new technologies to help automate tasks and free up bandwidth to get into flow. We are focused on getting on the donut and in the learning zone. Ultimately, flow is not about disengaging but rather about finding ways to heighten our focus in an increasingly information rich world. Flow, in this sense, is not about shutting down. It's about finding ways to modulate the specific channels to which we are attentive. This means that in flow there doesn't need to be sacrifice or compromise, but rather a commitment to being present and focused on the tasks, people, and outcomes that matter most.

This is where your own commitment to flow continues. Take time out to identify the goals you want to pursue and to set realistic timeframes for tackling these endeavors. Know why you are dedicating yourself to achieving these goals. Then, take stock of what may be holding you back. What habits in your life are obstacles and which ones are already helping you optimize and engage more deeply?

How can you harness these productive habits to further optimize? How can you leverage these habits to build a finely tuned system to excel in all aspects of your work and life? Don't forget that the most powerful quality of flow is that flow begets more flow. Once you discover flow, creating more flow will become second nature.

GLOSSARY

Bandwidth usually refers to the rate at which data is transferred. In flow, bandwidth is one's capacity or ability to hold and process information or your ability to focus on the things that matter most.

Donut is this book's preferred metaphor for describing how to get into flow. Life *inside* the donut hole is our comfort zone. It is safe, familiar, comfortable, and potentially a little boring. Life on the donut is our learning zone. This is where we grow, stretch, and experiment. This is where we feel alive, inspired, and awake. This is also where we struggle as we push ourselves. The edge of the donut is the outer edge of the learning zone. Too much time on the outer edge—in what might be called terror's edge—and we feel stressed. If we never go to the outer edge, however, we are failing to take enough risks. Flow happens when we are in the learning zone or on the donut. This is where we have clear goals that are challenging but not paralyzing.

Flow happens when we are focused, energized, and at our peak of creativity. In flow, we are performing at our best and our synapses are firing on every level. Flow is a truly absorbing experience that makes us feel in control even when under pressure. When we are in flow we lose track of time, and actions appear to be guided by an inner logic. One of the most amazing aspects of flow is that it is rewarding in itself.

Grit is a personal quality identified by psychologist Angela Duckworth. It is about having the perseverance and passion to pursue long-term goals, even if and when the going gets tough!

Hacking entails finding solutions to problems and challenges no matter how banal or profound they may be. You can hack your daily life by automating your grocery deliveries. You can hack your work by learning how to effectively delegate. You can hack your relationship by developing ways to avoid conflicts and increase communication. The goal of hacking is to get the desired outcome in the fastest, easiest, most cost-effective way possible.

Preparation is vital to optimize one's likelihood for flow. In preparation, we are establishing goals: associated projects or subtasks, creating optimal conditions, collecting essential resources, and assembling our team.

Purposeful struggle is about moving toward a goal with focus and energy. It is the heavy lifting associated with learning new skills, developing capabilities and moving the dial on major projects.

Recovery is the final stage of flow. The neurochemical high of the flow state is often followed by a darker, drained low state. As the surge of neurochemicals fade, we are often left with a funky set of emotions. Letting ourselves recover, and recover fully, is critical.

Release is the third stage of flow. Research shows that we can only struggle intentionally, purposefully and with full effort in small intervals (at most, in 90-minute sprints). To maximize the impact of our struggle, we need to stop struggling from time to time and release during short periods of rest.

Self-awareness is about knowing yourself—your triggers and your goals. In short, self-awareness is about having a personal user manual and following it and updating it on a regular basis.

Triggers are conditions, situations or experiences that have a profound impact on us (positive or negative). For whatever reason, some stimuli can move us to step up and be magnificent and other stimuli can reduce us to tears. Knowing your triggers, both good and bad, is vital for setting yourself up to be in the best possible position to achieve and maintain flow.

Wired refers to our current state — the state of being constantly connected via digital technologies to our work, friends, family and the world. If we are *overwired*, we're distracted and depleted. If we are *rewired*, we have found a way to hack this 21st-century problem.

REFERENCES

1. Jeanne Nakamura and Mihaly Csikszentmihalyi, "Flow Theory and Research," *The Oxford Handbook of Positive Psychology* (2nd Edition), Eds. Shame J. Lopez and C.R. Snyder (Oxford: Oxford University Press, 2009).

2. Steven Engeser and Falco Rheinberg, "Flow, performance and moderators of challenge-skill balance," *Motivation and Emotion* 3, (2008):158.

3. Mihaly Csikszentmihalyi and Asakawa, "Universal and Cultural Dimensions of Optimal Experiences," *Japanese Psychological Research* (January 2016).

4. Ibid.

5. Guy Cheron. "How to Measure the Psychological "Flow"? A Neuroscience Perspective." *Frontiers in Psychology* 7, (2016):1823.

6. Deloitte, 2016 *Global Mobile Consumer Survey*. https://www2. deloitte.com/us/en/pages/technology-media-and-telecommunications/ articles/global-mobile-consumer-survey-us-edition.html.

7. Angus Deaton and Daniel Kahneman, "High Income Improves evaluation of life but not emotional well-being," Proceedings of the National Academy of Science, Vol. 107, No. 38 (2010).

8. MetLife, *The American Dream: The Do-It-Yourself Dream* (2011), https://www.metlife.com/assets/institutional/services/ insights-and-tools/ml-2011-american-dream-report.pdf.

9. Tim Kasser, *The High Price of Materialism* (Cambridge: The MIT Press, 2002).

10. Diane Mulcahy, *The Gig Economy* (New York: American Management Association, 2017): 196-197.

11. Carol Dweck, *Mindset* (New York: Random House, 2006).

12. Ibid.

13. Angela Duckworth, *Grit* (New York: Simon & Schuster, 2016): 269.

14. Find out where you rank on Angela Duckworth's "Grit Scale" by visiting her website: http://angeladuckworth.com/grit-scale/.

15. Alan Deutschman, "Change or Die," *Fast Company* (May 1, 2005).

16. Daniel Goleman, "How Emotional Intelligence Matters," http://www.danielgoleman.info/ how-emotional-intelligence-matters/.

17. Pavlov knew that there were at least a few things that dogs never needed to learn, including how to salivate when they see food. This is a hardwired reflex or unconditioned response. Pavlov discovered that any object or event that his dogs associated with food (e.g., a lab assistant walking into the room but without food) could also trigger this response. The lesson is simple: There are multiple ways to "trigger" hardwired reflexes.

18. Adam Grant, "Why I Taught Myself to Procrastinate," *The New York Times* (January 16, 2016): SR1.

19. Tony Schwartz, "Manage Your Energy, Not Your Time," *Harvard Business Review* (October 2007).

ACKNOWLEDGMENTS

The creation of this book has been a journey shared by many people, and I hope the result is an adventure many more people will share.

While writing *Create More Flow*, life got busy. The busier life got, the more ideas percolated. Uncle Phil and Mom, I'm glad you are out of the woods, and I am grateful to have shared your health journeys. You remind me of what a blessing it is to have passion, especially when navigating adversity. Dad, although you have been gone more than two years, you still feel close and continue to inspire me to be better every day.

Susan and Edie, your foresight in creating the Grove Sisterhood has blessed me every day. Ivy, thank you for your passing comment (5.16.14) that haunted me into action! I also wish to thank the early adopters who nudged me forward (especially, Amy), the eager learners who came back for more (including Miriam, Mark, and Nancy), and the sisters who were beside me throughout the journey. I'm especially grateful to Ramya for miles of talks and for hearing my dreams, Mary Pat for the sage wisdom, Sarah for the systems insights over the years, Terry and Melissa for the sanctuary of your home (and hot tub) to complete the first draft of this book, and Joanne for the clarity of your process, crisp guidance, and loving friendship that made this book 500 times easier and more fun to write. Thank you to all my sisters on this adventure.

And to my inner circle: Bill and Bob, your witty validation energizes me. Ryan, your laughter on demand and witty friendship, especially on the darker days, kept me churning forward, giving me something to ski for. Courtney, you have been an unwavering ballast who has consistently delivered bandwidth, sanity, thought partnership, and coveted life wisdom. Cait, you are a wizard with words, a force for good, and a truly awe-inspiring collaborator.

To Adie and Pres, you make me crave flow and the capacity be fully present. Your laughter and snuggles fill my soul. Finally, Mark, thank you for your unconditional love, your persistent participation in the accelerators, your gentle nudging, and for changing all those extra diapers so I could focus.

ABOUT DR. CAMILLE PRESTON

Dr. Camille Preston is a leadership expert. She understands where people are, what is happening to them, and how to support their efforts to self-optimize. Dr. Preston specializes in helping people unlock their capacity for excellence, action, and impact. Her clients learn to lead — and live — more effectively. A psychologist by training, she is particularly skilled at recognizing the underlying patterns that inhibit performance. She works with individuals and teams to identify specific actions they can take to amplify impact.

The author of *Rewired* (2011), Dr. Preston is also a thought leader in the tech-mindfulness movement. She is known nationwide as an expert on virtual effectiveness. Executives turn to her to discover how to leverage technology, rewire for results, and create impactful, effective collaborations with people in a networked world. In *Create More Flow*, Dr. Preston leverages her deep knowledge and experience to offer readers a toolkit for self-optimization at work and in life.